# MARSHALL PASS

## Denver & Rio Grande Gateway to the Gunnison Country

### FEATURING THE DOW HELMERS COLLECTION

WALTER R. BORNEMAN

WESTERN REFLECTIONS PUBLISHING COMPANY®
Lake City, Colorado

© Copyright 1980, 2020 by Walter R. Borneman
All rights reserved in whole or in part

ISBN 978-1-937851-50-7

Second Edition
Printed in the United States

Front cover painting by Howard Fogg and back cover painting by Jan Rons courtesy of the Al and Lynne Dunton Collection.

Cover and Text Design by Laurie Casselberry
Laurie Goralka Design

Western Reflections Publishing Company
P. O. Box 1149
951 N. Highway 149
Lake City, Colorado 81235
www.westernreflectionspublishing.com
(970) 944-0110

## DEDICATION

*To my grandparents, Walter and Hazel Borneman, with love and fond memories of many a childhood evening spent down at the depot watching the trains come in, and to Dow Helmers, who instilled in us the love and appreciation we have for Colorado's majestic mountains and the little trains that labored through them. We treasure the many happy hours we spent exploring.*

# Preface

Things that are meant to be seem to have a way of defying odds and falling into place. This is certainly the case of this book about Marshall Pass and how it has come into being.

My husband, Dow Helmers, was involved in numerous projects during his busy and productive life, and while he was able to follow to completion many of these projects, one major effort remained incomplete at the time of his death in 1976. For years, he spent endless hours researching old documents, collecting photographs, and photographing Marshall Pass. The completion of this project would have been the realization of his finest effort. As a result of those years of painstaking labor, he left behind boxes of notes, interviews, maps, and hundreds of photographs of this famed railroad pass.

Not wanting Dow's fine collection of material to be left incomplete and realizing that something should be done to preserve the fruits of his labors, I mentioned the collection to Leland Feitz, a publisher and long-time friend of Dow's. After reviewing the material, he also agreed that something must be done to preserve this valuable collection. With this decided, we set out to find answers to the many things that needed to be done. The most pressing and important was to find someone to complete the job.

Then fate played its hand!

During the spring of 1978, Al Dunton, a Fort Collins publisher-friend of Leland's, stopped in Colorado Springs for the night. The following morning, they met for an unscheduled breakfast. As talk turned to publishing, Al mentioned that he had a manuscript about Marshall Pass, written by a young Colorado author, Walter Borneman. The only things lacking were photographs and some "personal" history. At this point, Leland told him of Dow's collection of research, interviews, and photographs.

The following day, Leland telephoned me concerning his previous day's conversation and arranged to bring Walter Borneman to my home. I immediately felt that Walt was the right person for the project we had in mind. As a dedicated young historian and gifted writer, it was obvious that he had a deep feeling for the history of the area. But, more important to me, he had a deep sensitivity for Dow and his work as a railroad historian.

I would never have shared Dow's treasured photographs and research with just anyone, but I certainly had no reservations about sharing them with Walt and Leland who both expressed such a total commitment to a project so dear to Dow's heart.

We all share a feeling of dedication to this book and we know it will be a fitting memorial to the man who first dreamed it should be done.

I especially wish to offer my gratitude to Leland for his help in getting this, as well as Dow's other works, accomplished.

Theresa Helmers  
Colorado Springs, Colorado  
April 1, 1980

# Foreword

Of all the Colorado narrow gauge routes that struggled over the state's Continental Divide, only the Marshall Pass line was a main line. This route made the Denver & Rio Grande truly a transcontinental. This was not a line to reach remote gold and silver camps, or coal mines, but a line reaching to Utah and connections to the Pacific.

The very names of the passenger trains of long ago indicated management's hope and pride—"Atlantic Express," "Pacific Express." Pride before long succumbed to practicality, and the change of cars to and from narrow gauge was a surprise not indicated by the timetable, a surprise to passengers, however generally enthusiastic of their trip.

Long after competition had forced the "Baby Road" to discard that nickname and construct a standard gauge route, the Marshall Pass line was recognized and advertised as an alternate main line across the state. The other narrow gauge routes remained as branch lines, but only Marshall Pass received the new engines, and the improvements to track in extensive fills, eased curves, and heavy rail.

It has been twenty-five years since trains last challenged the slopes of Mount Ouray. It is no doubt a dramatic change for motorists now to master that winding cindery path. The aspens are just as pretty in fall as when they enchanted those who rode the Tuscan red coaches long ago. Perhaps we should look upon the railroad era as just a phase in transition of travel, from Mears's toll road to the present. But what a phase it was! — passenger trains in sections, excursionists from as far as Boston, freights day and night with three, even four engines, snowbound trains, and struggling flangers and rotaries to the rescue. The forested slopes hide a litter of tell-tale fragments from numerous long forgotten runaways and wrecks, from the legendary days of link and pin and straight air brakes.

Fortunately the camera recorded some of these events. Did any of those trainmen and passengers ever think that someday "their" pass would be the subject of a book? Probably not; but I'm sure they would enjoy this volume.

Robert W. Richardson  
Colorado Railroad Museum

## Acknowledgments

Just as engineers needed brave and faithful firemen and brakemen to shepherd their trains across Marshall Pass, so too, do authors need a great many people to help them in their journey. During the research and writing of the history of Marshall Pass, Dow Helmers and I were aided immeasurably by a great number of people who contributed to its successful completion. Research assistance was graciously provided by Maxine Benson and the staff of the Colorado Historical Society, Eleanor Gehres and the staff of the Western History Department of the Denver Public Library, and the staff of the Charles L. Tutt Library of Colorado College. A special thanks must go to Mrs. Olive R. Gifford and the staff of the Leslie J. Savage Library, Western State College. For two years I could not walk through Savage Library without Mrs. Gifford waving a sheet of paper containing another "lead" on Marshall Pass.

Dr. William D. Edmondson and Professor Abbott Fay of Western State College and Allen H. Dunton of Centennial Publications also provided valuable advice and encouragement and commented on the completed drafts. Will Hook and Leland Feitz of Century One Press were cooperative and enthusiastic publishers and deserve sincere thanks for their many contributions to the final product.

The many people who gave of their time to both Dow and myself in interviews are graciously acknowledged throughout the text and here: From the Dow Helmers Collection: Merle Gregg, William Crylie, Ted McDowell, Frank Veo, Margaret Hendricks, Gus Latham, Bill Ausmus, and R. F. Camblin; and from my collection, Rivers Edgar Banks, Merle Brown, Rial Lake, Dr. Kenneth Lampert, and Deal W. Richardson.

A major portion of this work is the substantial photograph collection of Dow Helmers. A very appreciative thank you is due the contributors to that collection: Robert W. Richardson, Jackson C. Thode, Neal R. Miller, Donald Duke, Charles Webb, James Ozment, Mrs. W. R. Thompson, Gerald M. Best, Richard B. Jackson, Richard Ronzio, Francis and Freda Rizzari, Leah Sandusky, Lacy Humbeutel, Glenn George, and Paul Brinkeroff.

Accolades of the highest order are due to Dow's good friend Robert W. Richardson of the Colorado Railroad Museum, not only for his superb photographic contributions, but for his critical reading and always helpful suggestions. My friend, colleague, and occasional co-author, Duane Vandenbusche, Professor of History at Western State College, deserves many thanks not only for originally interesting me in Marshall Pass, but also for sharpening and honing my historical skills over the years. As always, Lyndon J. Lampert, my co-author in *A Climbing Guide to Colorado's Fourteeners*, generously provided yeoman's service of the most useful kind.

My deep thanks go also to my companion of many mountains and many trails, R. Omar Richardson, who viewed the pass with me from jeep, skis, and airplane, and on one occasion, with our friends, Gary and Dolora Koontz, braved twenty-four miles of cold skiing to photograph the pass in winter.

My greatest debt, of course, is to Dow and Theresa Helmers. The Dow Helmers Collection of research, photographs, and interviews provided the golden thread with which to tie my manuscript together and the locomotive power needed to boost it over the pass. Throughout the combining of the results of Dow's labors and mine, Mrs. Helmers has been a most gracious and enthusiastic partner; it has been a joy to work with her and realize this memorial to Dow's memory.

Walter R. Borneman<br>June 12, 1980

# Contents

|     | Introduction: Keys to Empire | 9 |
| --- | --- | --- |
| I | From Toothache to Wagon Ruts | 11 |
| II | The Coming of the Rails | 23 |
| III | Cornerstone of An Empire | 45 |
| IV | A Wooden Railroad Run by Iron Men | 81 |
| V | "There's Something About Railroading That A Man Enjoys" | 103 |
| VI | Tunnels, Highways, and Fading Whistles | 117 |
|     | Epilogue: A Glorious Past, An Uncertain Future | 167 |
|     | Selected Bibliography | 171 |
|     | Index | 174 |

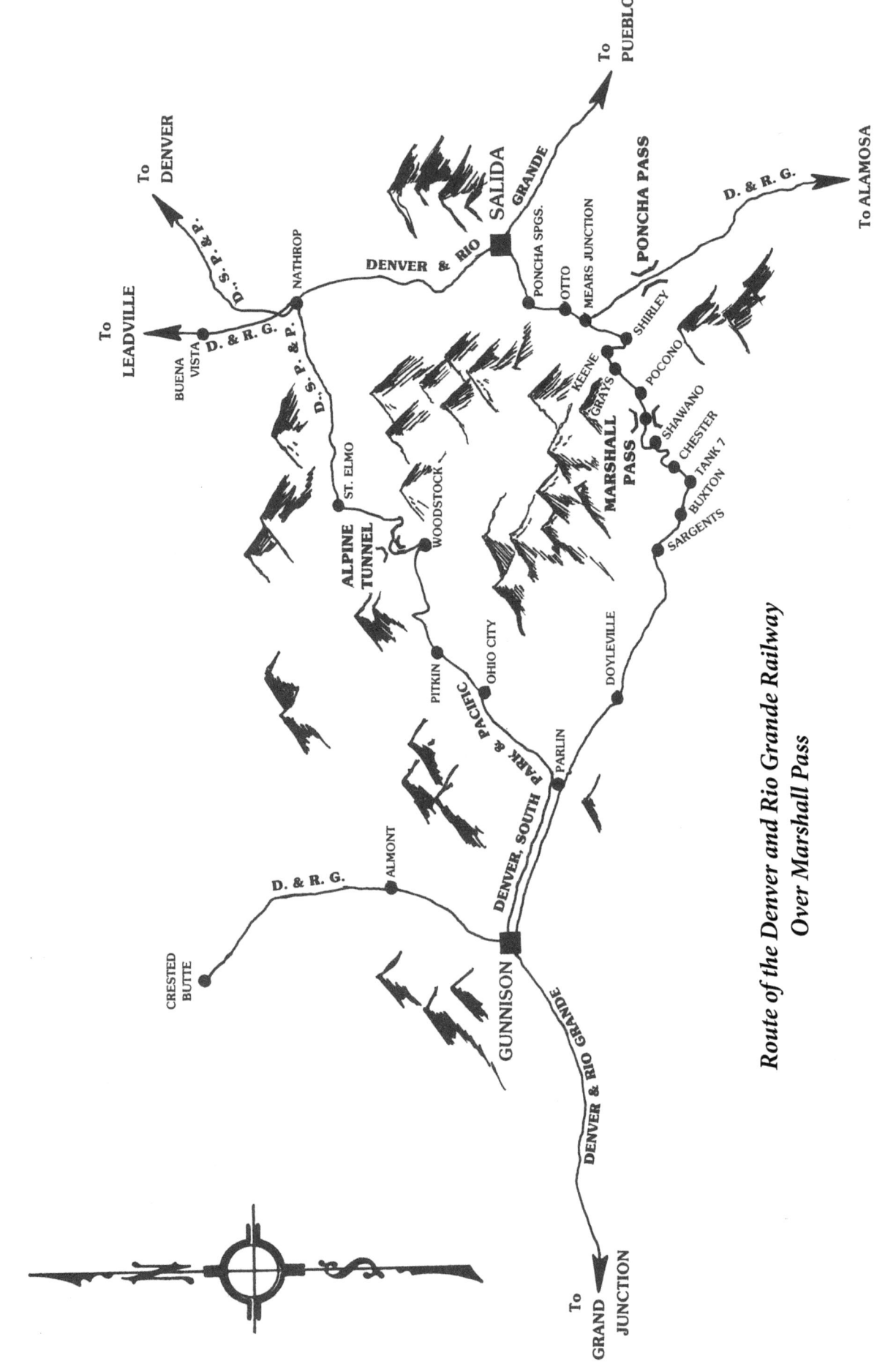

*Route of the Denver and Rio Grande Railway Over Marshall Pass*

# Introduction: Keys To Empire

As American settlers slowly trudged their way westward across the Great Plains during the nineteenth century, they were confronted with the towering barrier of the Rocky Mountains. Rising to over 14,000 feet and stretching more than 1,200 miles from Canada to New Mexico, the high reaches of this granite uplift serve not only as the backbone of the North American continent, but also as one of the few rapidly disappearing sanctuaries of natural resources and beauty. Majestic, treacherous, awe inspiring, disgusting, the Rockies held the dreams of many, and many came to seek their resolution. There were railroad moguls like William Jackson Palmer and John Evans, mining tycoons like H. A. W. Tabor and Winfield Scott Stratton, enterprising entrepreneurs like Otto Mears and Marshall Field, and always the common man, McIntosh, Schroeder, Zabrusky, Costanzo, Romero, and Brontman, the men who made the opening of the land possible with hard work and sweat.

To the men heading west, the Rockies lay as a giant maze, a land of labyrinthine valleys and mountains, whose inner secrets were guarded by great ranges of towering, snow-capped sentinels. Fortunately for the pioneers there were keys which permitted passage through the barriers. The Rocky Mountain passes, which were indeed, as Marshall Sprague has called them, "The Great Gates," offered the keys needed to unlock the riches and beauty that lay within the labyrinth. Since elements of Coronado's army first looked over Glorieta Pass in central New Mexico in 1540, the story of the opening of the great American West has been the story of the discovering and conquering of the great gates. Juan Bautista de Anza, Spanish Governor of New Mexico, rode north in 1779 and crossed over Poncha Pass from the drainage of the Rio Grande River to the drainage of the Arkansas River in central Colorado, while chasing Comanche raiders under Cuerno Verde. Jim Bridger and the mountain men of the 1820s pioneered routes over South Pass, which became the gateway for the Oregon Trail. The rush to Texas and the southwest of the 1830s and 1840s brought a swelling of trade hurrying over Sangre de Cristo Pass and Raton Pass between Bent's Fort on the Arkansas River and Santa Fe, New Mexico. By the time of the Treaty of Guadalupe Hidalgo in 1848 and the beginnings of the California gold rush the following year, the bubble of westward expansion had burst wide open and men rushed by the thousands over the next pass into the next valley searching for their El Dorado.

By May of 1869, the driving of the golden spike in the first transcontinental railroad at Promontory, Utah, signalled the dawning of a new era in the history of the passes. Railroads with energetic men at their helms, eager to reap the profits of new areas, fought to control the strategic passes as routes into the new territories. Few areas could match the frenzy of the rushes to the mineral belts and equally few could match the fierce competition of the railroads that Colorado experienced in the 1870s. Having been beaten by the Santa Fe Railroad in its attempt to cross Raton Pass en route to El Paso, the Denver and Rio Grande Railway turned its tracks to the west, wrestled control of the Royal Gorge away from the Santa Fe, and raced for the bustling silver mining center of Leadville.

As Leadville boomed, a new area came into the news; the Gunnison country west of the Continental Divide whispered of becoming another Leadville. William Jackson Palmer's Denver and Rio Grande and John Evans's Denver, South Park, and Pacific hungrily eyed the prize and made plans to add another vein to their rapidly spreading network of railroad arteries. So it was that in the opening years of the 1880s the wagon ruts over Marshall Pass were joined by ribbons of steel, as the Denver and Rio Grande Railway fought its way westward in its drive to build an empire.

# FROM TOOTHACHE TO WAGON RUTS

*The sweeping grandeur of the Continental Divide, as seen from the summit of 11,655-foot Methodist Mountain. Chipeta Peak is at right, Mount Ouray, at center. Marshall Pass threads its way past the left (south) shoulder of Mount Ouray.*
DOW HELMERS COLLECTION

# 1
# From Toothache to Wagon Ruts

*The opening of the Marshall Pass toll road will be a source of gratification and an event of no small magnitude in the prosperity of the Gunnison and San Juan counties.*
— *Gunnison Review,* June 5, 1880

*The efficient general manager of the D&RGRR, Gen. D. C. Dodge was in the city last week in the interest of the popular road he represents. We understand he was here to examine the practicability of a railway line via Marshall Pass to the Gunnison country.*
— *Gunnison Review,* June 19, 1880

Marshall Pass is located on the Continental Divide in central Colorado seventeen miles southwest of Salida at an elevation of 10,846 feet. Geographically, a pass is a low point in a ridge which separates two watersheds; in the case of Marshall Pass, the waters of Poncha Creek flowing east from the crest of the Divide eventually join the Arkansas River, while the waters of Marshall Creek flowing west from its crest eventually become a part of the Gunnison River. To the north the mighty Sawatch Range with fifteen peaks over 14,000 feet parallels the Continental Divide several miles to the east, while to the south the Divide swings southwest to circle the San Luis Valley and takes in a portion of the San Juan Mountains.

Marshall Pass nestles under the south shoulder of 13,971-foot Mount Ouray, named after the famed Ute Indian chief. The cirque which marks the mountain's east face and the ridges which come off the summit to the northeast and southeast resemble a huge chair, thus creating the legend that the spirit of Chief Ouray sits on this mountain ever watchful to what occurs beneath him. While it is probable that some of Ouray's ancestors used the pass that now lies at his feet, its recorded history began with a toothache in the mouth of the man who gave it its name.

William Louis Marshall was born on June 11, 1846, in Washington, Kentucky, the son of Colonel Charles A. and Phoebe Marshall and the grandson of Thomas Marshall, a brother of the famed Chief Justice. After attending the grammar school of Kenyon College, Marshall joined the 10th Kentucky Cavalry and fought for the Union in the Civil War for a year before being appointed to West Point in 1864. Upon his graduation in 1868, he was commissioned a second lieutenant in the Corps of Engineers with the prospect of a drab career in the peacetime army. His future brightened, however, in 1872, when he was assigned to the Wheeler Survey of the Rocky Mountains.[1]

George Montague Wheeler graduated from West Point two years before Marshall and by 1869 had convinced General A. A. Humphreys, the Chief of the Corps of Engineers, of the need for a survey of the West which would provide the army with information which was not being provided by the civilian surveys of John Wesley Powell and Ferdinand Vandeveer Hayden. By the time Marshall joined the Wheeler Survey, officially the United States Geographical Surveys West of the One Hundredth Meridian, General Humphreys had approved a plan by which Wheeler would map the entire West in a methodical project which would take fifteen years and cost $2,500,000. Although the formation of the United States Geological Survey in 1878 combined all of the individual surveys and brought the Wheeler expedition to a halt, Richard Bartlett, in his definitive study of the surveys, *Great Surveys of the American West*, suggested that if for no other reason, the Wheeler Survey was a success because of the lasting influence of a toothache experienced by William Marshall in the fall of 1873.[2]

Marshall was in command of one of three surveying parties that were operating in the Colorado division of the Wheeler Survey in 1873. His party had spent the summer and fall surveying in the San Juan Mountains near present-day Silverton. They were making plans to return to Denver before the worst of the winter set in when Marshall came down with what he later described as "one of the worst toothaches that ever befell a mortal." His mouth became so sore and swollen that he could not open it or even move his jaw, the result being that he was forced to live on very thin gruel. Being disenchanted with the prospect of a blacksmith extracting the tooth, Marshall made plans to reach the nearest dentist in Denver, three hundred miles away, as quickly as possible.

It was decided that the main party would follow the beaten path over Cochetopa Pass, which crosses the Continental Divide some sixty miles northeast of Silverton. The pain of Marshall's toothache made the circuitous nature of this route in the upper reaches of the San Luis Valley seem too long to bear, so he chanced on finding a more direct way through the mountains. With riding mules and one pack mule, Marshall set off with a packer named Dave Mears (no relation to Otto Mears) with the thought of attempting to get through the area of Twin Lakes in the central Sawatch Range. When heavy snows blocked his way in that direction, he remembered having seen another depression in the Divide and started toward the pass that would soon bear his name.

*William Marshall was a young lieutenant in the Corps of Engineers when he stumbled across the pass that today bears his name. Unfortunately, no picture can be found of Marshall in his early days of surveying the West. This photo shows the "Godfather of Marshall Pass" as a brigadier general many years after his discovery.* USMA ARCHIVES

While there was an abundance of snow, there was not quite so much as in other parts of the range and Marshall and Mears made a slow but steady advance each day. Slowed by fallen timber, deep snow, and fierce winds on the pass itself, they spent six days traveling the twelve miles near the top. Once on top of the pass, realizing that he had stumbled onto a possible east to west route, Marshall momentarily shook off the pain of his toothache and decided to spend a day and a night on the summit to make a survey of the pass. A keen geographer despite his pain, Marshall used his barometer and thermometer to take readings and to make a chart of the altitude and grade of the pass. So accurate were Marshall's measurements that a scant eight years later the Denver and Rio Grande Railway would use them with but a few alterations to build their line across the pass.

The night that Marshall and Dave Mears spent on the pass was certainly not the most pleasant of their lives. A low table of solid rock runs along the crest of the pass and the lee side offered some protection against the fierce westerly wind as Marshall and Mears faithfully took observations. Their measurements completed, they pushed on to Denver arriving four days before the main party despite the obstacles they encountered. Marshall found that the pass had saved them 125 miles. This fact, plus Marshall's assertion that a railroad could easily be built over the gentle slopes of the pass, caused much excitement in Denver and Marshall became a local celebrity, although he undoubtedly did not celebrate until he had promptly visited a dentist and had his famous toothache relieved.[3] While it is hard to estimate how rapidly news of the discovery of the new pass spread, it is almost a certainty that the information was greeted with particular interest by a short gentleman who spoke with a slight Russian accent as he roamed the streets of the growing supply center of Saguache at the head of the San Luis Valley.

Otto Mears, destined to become "The Pathfinder of the San Juans," was born on May 3, 1840, in Kurland, Russia,[4] the son of an English father and a Russian mother. Both of his parents died before he turned four and he was passed among relatives until he at last arrived in San Francisco at the age of ten, planning to live with an uncle. Unknown to Otto, the uncle had since left for Australia but Mears was befriended by the owner of a boarding house who got him a job selling newspapers.

In 1859, at the age of nineteen, he went to work in the mining camps of California and Nevada and two years later joined the First Regiment of the California Volunteers of the Union Army. After three years of service in Arizona and New Mexico, Mears settled in the lower San Luis Valley and within a year after his discharge became the proprietor of a store, gristmill, sawmill, and wheat farm. Indeed, this orphaned immigrant was not one to let things stand in his way. When wheat prices fell at Fort Garland, Mears hauled his wheat up the San Luis Valley, over Poncha Pass, and on to the still quiet mining town of Leadville.

Perhaps on one of these trips over Poncha Pass, as Mears urged his mules up the grade, he looked toward the Continental Divide a half dozen miles to the west and noticed the depression in the ridge where William Marshall would soon spend a restless night. It is certain that on one such trip he met former territorial governor William Gilpin, who urged him to pay the necessary five dollar charter fee to the territorial legislature and to construct a toll road over Poncha Pass. Gilpin advised him to construct a road that would not only serve as a wagon road, but also would have a gentle enough grade for a future railroad. Mears did just that and constructed a fifty-mile toll road from Saguache over Poncha Pass to Nathrop on the Arkansas River where it connected with a road toward Leadville. From this first venture in 1867 until 1886, Mears constructed a dozen major toll roads in southwestern Colorado and became one of the most influential businessmen of the region.[5] It was one of these enterprises that brought him to Marshall Pass.

*Otto Mears, "The Pathfinder of the San Juans," built a transportation empire in southwest Colorado. The Mears system of toll roads served to open the San Juan Mountains to mining and eventual settlement. Many of his toll roads, such as the Marshall Pass Road, later became routes for railroads.*   P. DAVID SMITH COLLECTION

On August 3, 1877, almost four years after Marshall's historic crossing, Otto Mears chartered the Marshall Pass and Gunnison Toll Road. The capital cost was $15,000 with $100 shares.[6] The road ran west from Mears Junction just north of Poncha Pass on Mears's Poncha Pass Toll Road, crossed Marshall Pass, and descended by way of Marshall Creek and Tomichi Creek to the budding supply center of Gunnison, a distance of about sixty miles. The distance of the road over the pass from Mears Junction at the base on the east side to the confluence of Marshall Creek and Tomichi Creek at the base on the west was approximately thirty-two miles.[7]

Work progressed slowly on the toll road and even by the fall of 1879 when the McKee family, who had spent the summer in Gunnison and were returning to Cañon City for the winter, used the road, they found it in poor condition. On many of the lower stretches there was no road at all, and it took a great deal of climbing over ridges, crossing creeks, and circling gulches to get through. The McKee outfit was the first four-horse team to cross the pass in either direction.[8]

Work on the pass increased during the spring of 1880 and by June 15 of that year W. M. Outcalt, the superintendent of the Marshall Pass work force, reported to the *Gunnison News* that the road was complete and that "all who travel it pronounce it the best road into the county."[9] Otto Mears, always the energetic businessman, heralded this accomplishment by running the following ad in the *Mountain Mail* of South Arkansas, soon to be called Salida:

> *If you are bound for the Gunnison, take the Marshall Pass Road. The route is now open, and is by thirty miles the shortest road to Gunnison City, Pitkin, Ruby Camp, Virginia City, Hillerton, Gothic, Crested Butte and all other points in the Gunnison Country. It is only 60 miles from South Arkansas to Gunnison City. This is the most direct route to Lake City, Ouray, San Miguel, and all points in the San Juan Country. Ship your freight in care of forwarding houses at South Arkansas, and thus avoid tedious delays that are caused by other routes.*         *Otto Mears*[10]

Otto Mears was not the only one announcing things to come with the opening of the Marshall Pass Road. The *Mountain Mail* of June 12, 1880, also reported that the Barlow and Sanderson Stage Company was inaugurating stage service between South Arkansas and Gunnison over Marshall Pass.[11] Barlow and Sanderson had entered into a partnership in 1860 to run stage lines west of Missouri. By 1866, they were running stages a distance of 2,450 miles from Kansas City to Los Angeles. Although referred to by many as Barlow and Sanderson, the firm was now technically J. L. Sanderson and Company and operated 2,400 miles of line in Colorado, New Mexico, Oregon, and California, using 125 coaches, 2,400 head of stock, and 1,000 men in a business that was rapidly coming to a close as the railroads rushed west.[12] The article of June 12 which boasted of bringing stage service to the Gunnison country stated that the stage left South Arkansas at 7:00 A. M. daily, one hour after the Denver and Rio Grande's overnight train from Denver arrived, and reached Gunnison at 7:00 P. M. that same evening. Indeed, it was noted, this one day service from Denver was sure to be a big boost to the Gunnison country.[13]

One important point must be emphasized if one is to understand the newspaper accounts of this era. Nothing gave rival editors greater pleasure than poking fun at a neighboring town while extolling the virtues of their own community. Almost every town which first boomed and had a newspaper was "destined" in the words of the editor to become most assuredly the "new capital of Colorado." Thus, it was this spirit of community "boosterism," unequalled by modern Chambers of Commerce, which was reflected by the newspapers of South Arkansas and Gunnison concerning the Marshall Pass Toll Road.

A week after the inauguration of stage service, the *Mountain Mail* reported that traffic over the pass was increasing steadily and that three Sanderson coaches had gone out on the 17th, two on the 18th, and two on the 19th, and that all were loaded to their fullest extent, which

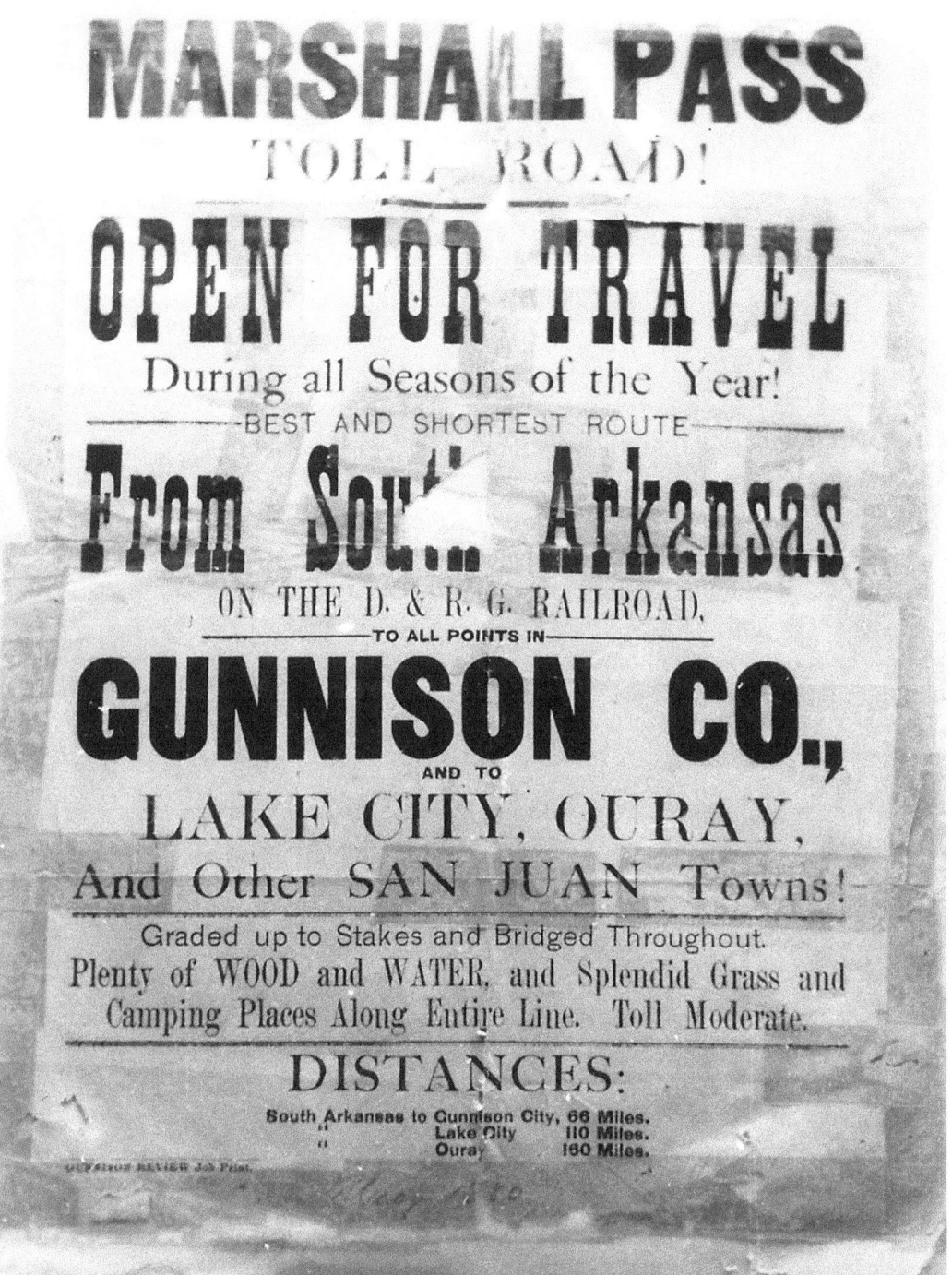

As the rush to the Gunnison country increased during the summer of 1880, Otto Mears had the Gunnison Review *print this ad extolling the virtues of his Marshall Pass Toll Road. Undoubtedly, there were those who would dispute his statement that the route was open "during all seasons of the year."*  WESTERN STATE COLLEGE LIBRARY

for the type of coaches employed at that time meant from eight to ten people. Not only was the stage business booming, declared the *Mail*, but in addition, some freighters were reporting the Marshall Pass Road to be the best crossing into the Gunnison country from any direction and that a great many wagons were on the road with freight.[14]

Meanwhile, in Gunnison, the editors of the *Gunnison News* lowered themselves to admitting that there had been "some" criticisms of the Marshall Pass Road, but that they had personally been over the road and could report it to be the "best, easiest, and quickest route between Gunnison and the railroad connection at South Arkansas."[15] By August 7, South Arkansas had become Salida, meaning "exit" in Spanish and referring to the sudden widening of the Arkansas River canyon. *The Mountain Mail* of that date did away with any reservations and stated that it was the "universal" verdict that the Marshall Pass Road was not only a good one, but the best in Colorado. It went on to point out that on other passes it sometimes required a good team just to haul an empty wagon up the grade, but that on Marshall Pass there were no such problems because of an easy grade all of the way.[16]

As the fall of 1880 approached, the *Gunnison Review* of September 11 wrote of the safety and speed of a pleasant trip to the east over Marshall Pass in one of J. L. Sanderson's stages. The road, the *Review* concluded, was doubtless the finest in Colorado with "one of the most careful and experienced drivers in the state holding the ribbons and taking you over the rugged scenery of Marshall Pass with six horses, making time at the rate of nearly ten miles an hour on the east slope."[17] If these were the conditions on the toll road from the newspapers' point of view, other people had different ideas of the quality of the road.

Betty Wallace, in *Gunnison Country*, a collection of stories and yarns of the settling years of the region, noted that all people did not find Mears's road to be "the finest in the state." It seems as though one day Mears stopped to exchange the time of day with a couple of unlucky travelers who had their wagons stuck fast in a mud hole on Marshall Pass. Mears listened sympathetically and anonymously as the men spoke a profaned and impassioned denunciation of any man who would dare to charge a toll for a road in such a condition as the one on which they were presently stuck. After Mears listened quietly to their woes, he told them that they would probably have the chance to meet Mears since he had seen the roadbuilder about ten miles back. With that, the "Pathfinder of the San Juans" rode on.

If Mears did indeed refuse to help the stranded gentlemen, he was paid back for his actions by the prank of one of the stage drivers. The driver, noting that Mears was the only occupant of his coach, lashed his horses into a run, managing to guide them so the coach wheels would pass over every stump, rock, and chuckhole in the road. "Mears took it all in stride and turned the joke on the driver by crawling from the stage at the end of the journey and remarking with a yawn and a stretch, 'I've had such a beau-u-tiful sleep.'"[18]

Another tale of crossing Marshall Pass, which suggests that the condition of the road was not all the newspapers said it was, was related by Carrie Adell Strahorn in her account of thirty years of traveling in the West, *Fifteen Thousand Miles By Stage*. At the time of Mrs. Strahorn's journey across the wilds of Marshall Pass in August of 1880, the Denver and Rio Grande Railway had reached Leadville, allowing the Sanderson stage line to replace the smaller stages on the Marshall Pass line with larger models previously used for the Leadville traffic. Consequently, to Mrs. Strahorn's utter dismay, there were seventeen passengers on the coach, eleven of whom sat on three seats inside while the remaining six climbed on the roof amid the usual assortment of baggage, mail, and express. Mrs. Strahorn's stage had scarcely rolled through Poncha Springs, a station five miles west of Salida at the foot of Poncha Pass, when a forecast was made as to what kind of day it might turn out to be:

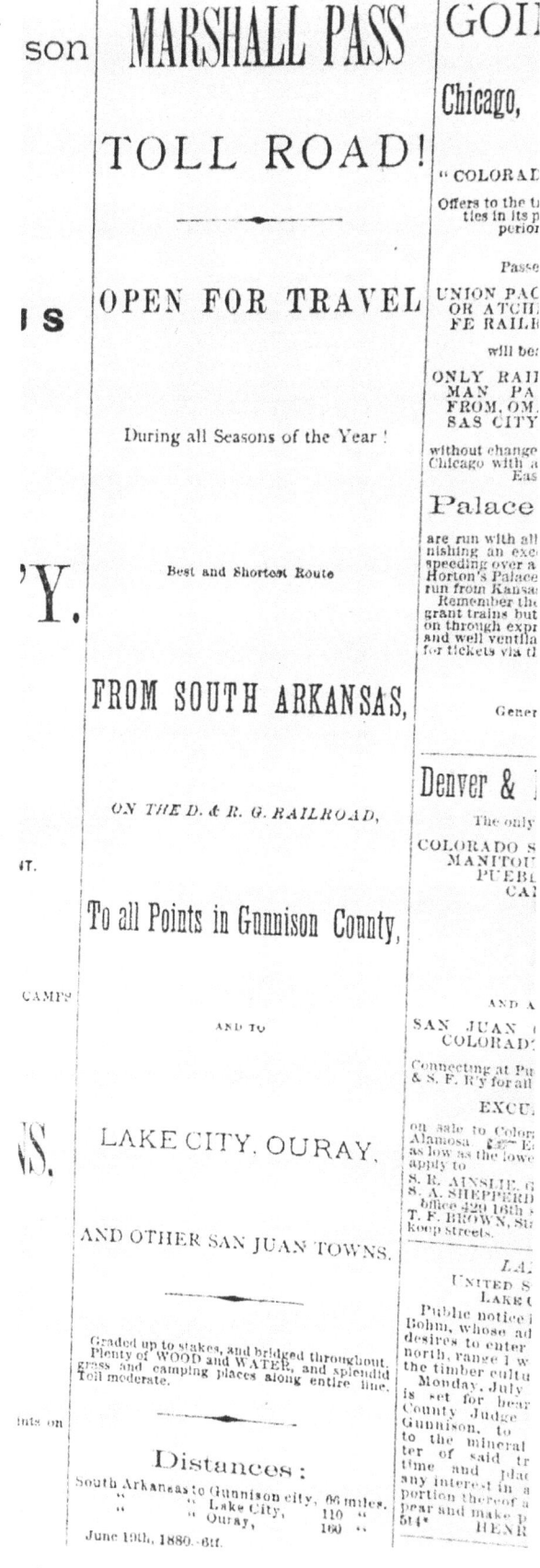

*This advertisement for the Marshall Pass Toll Road first appeared in the* Gunnison Review *on June 19, 1880.*

"*Graded up to stakes and bridged throughout. Plenty of wood and water and splendid grass and camping places along entire line. Toll moderate.*" So advertised Otto Mears about his Marshall Pass Toll Road, in June of 1880.
DENVER PUBLIC LIBRARY, WESTERN HISTORY COLLECTION, DOW HELMERS COLLECTION

> *The motion of the coach soon made two of the passengers very ill. There was no help for them, but they made plenty of discomfort for the rest of us. I was riding backward on the front seat and a man and a woman on the respective ends of the seat facing me had their heads out of the window incessantly to dispose of last week's ration, and there was but little cessation the whole day.*[19]

Between Poncha Springs and Gunnison the road followed the north side of all the valleys and it did not help Mrs. Strahorn's calmness any to note that the road was consistently slanted down the mountainside. A little farther up the pass one of the rear wheels of the stage struck a boulder and came close to upsetting the stage as two of the men on the roof lost their balance and went flying into a ravine. But then, no reason to panic about such things; the day was still young.

> *It was not long before the driver ran too close to the mountainside, when there was a steep pitch and again we were saved from destruction by one of the heaviest men grabbing a well-rooted sapling and holding it fast until the wheels dropped to a level again.*
>
> *A little farther on we locked wheels with a freight wagon and turned the wagon over, spilling its contents to an accompaniment of profuse bad language of the freighter, and we delayed long enough for our passengers to help the man gather his load again. This is not the place, although it may be the time, to repeat what the freighter's remarks were about the accident, but we hastened away without writing them down.*[20]

After a good dinner to replenish the six o'clock breakfast, which by then had become a dream, the travelers reboarded the stage to hear the driver remark that he was now in a hurry as there were several spots he wanted to get over before dark. As the stage bounced and jerked toward Gunnison, Mrs. Strahorn heard a seasoned pioneer remark, "I am no tenderfoot, but an old mountaineer, used to danger and exposure, but this trip beats all, and my thoughts have been with home and God all day."[21] As the driver urged his horses over the rapidly darkening road the air was occasionally interrupted by his cry of "to the right" and the passengers would quickly lean in that direction until the stage had passed the bad stretch and resumed a level posture. After a narrow escape from such a situation a strange hush fell over the coach.

> *The quiet was finally broken by another warning from the driver, and we all leaned to the north, but our time had come, and in spite of all efforts we went over rattle-ty-bang-smash crash, coach, bodies, baggage, mail, treasure box, and tools, in a heap and all in the dark.*[22]

After a hurried inventory of bumps and bruises, several hours were spent accounting for the baggage that was scattered over the countryside. This done, the stage was righted and the journey toward Gunnison resumed. Noting that nothing could have tempted her to make a return journey to Poncha Springs and Salida by way of the pass unless on horseback or afoot, Mrs. Strahorn alighted from the coach in Gunnison, gave a quick, searching glance at the Gunnison Hotel to be certain it would stand the night, and then hastened to the quiet of her room for a few hours of well-deserved rest.[23]

Now that both sides have been heard from, it would seem that actual conditions on the toll road over Marshall Pass in 1880 were somewhere between the picture painted by the fiery boosterism of the local newspapers and the over-dramatic remembrances of a Victorian lady whose reminiscences undoubtedly adhered to the principle that the book account is always written more dramatically than the life experience. Indeed, this is not meant to belittle the hardships and the sacrifices that needed to be made to move westward and settle a new area. It took hardy men to move freight across a road more than two miles above sea level and to endure the bitter and fickle weather which is so characteristic of Colorado's Continental Divide. The history of Marshall Pass is scattered with the names of celebrities who travelled over the pass. Ex-president U. S. Grant rode over the pass from Salida in a four horse Sanderson stage on his way to visit the mining towns north of Gunnison as early as July of 1880.[24] However, it was the common man whose name has long since been forgotten who led the rush over the pass into the Gunnison country.

Gunnison City served as the impetus for the great rush of wagons over Marshall Pass in 1880 and 1881. Founded in 1874 by Sylvester Richardson, Gunnison in 1880 lay as the hub of the wheel of a great mining area. Never destined to become another Leadville, it instead boomed as the supply point for such silver camps as Ruby, Irwin, Tincup, Gothic, Lake City, White Pine, and Ouray. Originally the best route into the Gunnison country had been over Cochetopa Pass, the pass which William Marshall had forsaken for a shorter route. In 1880, with the Denver and Rio Grande Railway in Salida, Marshall Pass and Otto Mears's toll road offered a direct and shorter lifeline of supply from the east, and with this encouragement and the demands for a point of supply in the center of the mining belt Gunnison grew rapidly.

As the rush to the Gunnison country continued, the Marshall Pass Toll Road gave Otto Mears a handsome return on his investments. Strangely enough, one of the few blanks in the Colorado Historical Society's collections concerns record books from toll roads; therefore, it is difficult to estimate the profits of the road over Marshall Pass and educated guesses must rely on other information. It is known that the established practice on all toll roads was to locate the toll gates at the crossing of streams or in canyons where it was impossible for people to bypass them. The geography of Marshall Pass was well suited to this principle. While riders on horseback might bypass the toll gates, wagons or large bands of stock simply had to stick to the trail.[25]

Another bit of information that suggests Mears's profits were high was the report by the *Solid Muldoon* of Ouray that Mears had been offered a rental of $175 a day for the road.[26] It would seem that this figure is astronomically high, and is probably a typographical error or a joke; the latter seems to be the case, particularly when one considers the character of the *Muldoon's* editor, David Day, a man who was known much more for his fantastic tales and biting sarcasm than for his reliable reporting of the news. Nevertheless, the volume of traffic crossing the pass and the rates Mears charged suggest that his gross for a day may have indeed approached this amount.

While Mears's profits remain a mystery, the *Gunnison News* of June 12, 1880, did furnish information as to the rates he charged. A wagon with a two-horse team was four dollars; a wagon with one horse was two dollars; a wagon with additional teams of horses was charged two dollars per additional team; loose stock and pack animals were twenty-five cents a head, and saddle animals were fifty cents each.[27] These charges allowed the traveler passage from Mears Junction, where the road branched off from the Poncha Pass Toll Road and started up Marshall Pass, on to Gunnison. As the wagons rolled over the pass in the autumn of 1880, more changes

*While the railroad later made this circuitous loop just above Shirley, in 1880, the Mears toll road ran west alongside Poncha Creek toward the summit.*
DOW HELMERS COLLECTION

were in store for Marshall Pass than just the coloring of the aspen leaves.

Gunnison was rapidly becoming a booming supply center with needs of even stronger ties to the east than the toll road could offer. In September of 1880, Colorado Senator Nathaniel P. Hill announced to the *Mountain Mail* that he had received notice from the Second Assistant Postmaster General that starting September 1, regular mail service would be provided between Salida and Gunnison over the pass.[28] A little over a month later on October 22, the first telegraph signal was clicked out from Gunnison to Denver over the pass. Addressed to Colorado Governor Frederick W. Pitkin, the telegram read: "The great and future great of Colorado make their first spark by electricity today. It is a day that may well be remembered by this, one of the most wonderful mining centers of the world, we greet you."[29]

But there were more things to be excited about than mail service and telegrams. The iron horse first entered Salida on its way north to Leadville in May of 1880, and once it reached the silver camp the following July it turned its head westward toward the riches of the Gunnison country. Now, in the autumn of 1880, it stood with a full head of steam straining on its tracks at Salida urging to be turned loose to race for the Gunnison country and create one of the most colorful chapters of railroad history.

---

[1] Gustav J. Fiebeger, "Marshall, William Louis," *Dictionary of American Biography*, 1933 ed., XII, p. 332.

[2] Richard Adams Bartlett, *Great Surveys of the American West* (Norman: University of Oklahoma Press, 1962), pp. 333-372.

[3] Thomas Dawson, "Godfather of Marshall Pass," *The Trail*, (September, 1920), pp. 8-10. (Based on a personal interview with William Marshall.)

[4] Leroy Hafen, "Otto Mears, 'Pathfinder of the San Juan,'" *The Colorado Magazine*, IX, No. 2 (March, 1932), p. 71.

[5] Wilson Rockwell, "Portrait in the Gallery, Otto Mears, Pathfinder of the San Juans," *Denver Westerners Brand Book*, XXX, 1967, pp. 3-24.

[6] D. H. Cummins, "A Social and Economic History of Southwestern Colorado, 1860-1948," (unpublished Ph.D. dissertation, University of Texas, 1951), p. 416.

[7] United States Geological Survey, *Montrose, Colorado*, (30' Sectional), 1966.

[8] Betty Wallace, *Gunnison Country* (Denver: Sage Books, 1960), p. 50.

[9] *Gunnison News*, June 19, 1880, p. 3.

[10] *Mountain Mail*, June 12, 1880, p. 2.

[11] *Ibid.*, June 12, 1880, p. 2.

[12] *Gunnison News*, June 12, 1880, p. 3.

[13] *Mountain Mail*, June 12, 1880, p. 2.

[14] *Ibid.*, June 19, 1880, p. 3.

[15] *Gunnison News*, June 12, 1880, p. 2.

[16] *Mountain Mail*, August 7, 1880, p. 2.

[17] *Gunnison Review*, September 11, 1880, p. 3.

[18] Wallace, *Gunnison Country*, pp. 52-53.

[19] Carrie Adell Strahorn, *Fifteen Thousand Miles By Stage* (New York: The Knickerbocker Press, 1915), p. 216.

[20] *Ibid.*, p. 216.

[21] *Ibid.*, p . 217.

[22] *Ibid.*, p. 217-18.

[23] *Ibid.*, pp. 218-20.

[24] Marshall Sprague, *The Great Gates, The Story of the Rocky Mountain Passes* (Boston: Little, Brown, and Company, 1964), p. 349.

[25] D. H. Cummins, "Toll Roads in Southwestern Colorado," *The Colorado Magazine*, XXIX, (April, 1952), p. 104.

[26] *Solid Muldoon*, May 28, 1880, p. 3.

[27] *Gunnison News*, June 12, 1880, p. 2.

[28] *Mountain Mail*, September 4, 1880, p. 3.

[29] *Gunnison News*, October 30, 1880, p. 2.

# II

# The Coming of the Rails

*General William Jackson Palmer was the founder and guiding light of the Denver and Rio Grande Railway during its early years. Always a shrewd businessman, Palmer saw the Royal Gorge and Marshall Pass as the cornerstones of his developing empire. This included not only the Rockies of central Colorado, but also a transcontinental link to Salt Lake City.*
COLORADO HISTORICAL SOCIETY

# II
## THE COMING OF THE RAILS

*I had a dream last evening while sitting in the gloaming at the car window. I mean a wide-awake dream. Shall I tell it to you?*

*I thought how fine it would be to have a little railroad a few hundred miles in length, all under one's own control with one's friends, to have no jealousies and contests and differing policies, but to be able to carry out unimpeded and harmoniously one's views, in regards to what ought and ought not be done.*
—From a letter written on January 17, 1870, from Salina, Kansas, by General William Jackson Palmer to his beloved "Queen," describing his "Utopian" railroad, the future Denver and Rio Grande Railway.

*It will be good news to every citizen of Gunnison to learn that the contracts have already been let for the building of the Denver & Rio Grande at once to this city. The time is limited to seven months, which will be the last of next April.*

*The unsurpassed richness of the Gunnison country, we presume, is one of the inducements that helps to bring "Colorado's Pet" to our city. Our citizens one and all, will unite with the* Review *in welcoming the advent of any road that will advance the interests of the Gunnison country and no road in the state has a warmer or more friendly interest for this section than the popular, wide-awake, plucky D & R G.*

*We shall await, with pleasure, the advent of the road here.*
— Gunnison Review, *September 25, 1880*

*For the first time since the world began the shrill whistle of the locomotive was sounded last Tuesday morning on the summit of Marshall Pass at an elevation of 10,500 feet above the level of the sea.*

*The Denver & Rio Grande deserves great credit and praise for the lively work they have done the past few months and for the progress they have made in climbing the Continental Divide. They are the first Colorado railroad corporation to cross the backbone of the continent, but being men of energy, nerve and perseverance, backed with untold wealth, they knew no such word as fail.*
— Gunnison Review, *June 25, 1881*

If William Marshall was its godfather and Otto Mears the impetus of its childhood, then William Jackson Palmer was the driving force which thrust the Marshall Pass route into adulthood and into its position as an integral part of the empire of the Denver and Rio Grande Railway. Today, in the heart of Colorado Springs at the junction of U. S. 24 and stately, tree-lined Nevada Avenue, Palmer is immortalized in bronze as he sits astride a horse and surveys the changes which have taken place since he rode the first Rio Grande train into town over a century and a half ago. To the average citizen of Colorado Springs, he is simply and anonymously "the man on the horse," but to history he was the father of Colorado Springs and the founder and guiding light of the Denver and Rio Grande Railway. Most significantly, he was a man whose remarkable influence on the development of the Rocky Mountain West is still being felt.

William Jackson Palmer was born in Leipsic, Delaware, on September 18, 1836, the son of John and Matilda Jackson Palmer. In 1842, the family moved to Philadelphia where Palmer attended grammar school and high school. His eagerness for advancement was obvious in 1856, when, at the age of twenty, he became the secretary and treasurer of the Westmoreland Coal Company, a position which undoubtedly gave him valuable knowledge of the coal industry when he was looking for fuel to run his locomotives. Two years later he started acquiring the administrative experience necessary to run a railroad by serving for three years as private secretary to J. Edgar Thomson, the president of the Pennsylvania Railroad.

With the coming of the Civil War in 1861, Palmer followed his conscience rather than his parents' Quaker religion and helped the Union form the 15th Pennsylvania Cavalry. He served with distinction with Generals Grant and Sherman in their campaigns in the Mississippi Valley and Deep South and emerged from the war a Brevet Brigadier General of Volunteers. Then, like many Civil War veterans, Palmer went west to seek a new life.[1]

The tide of western expansion that would soon sweep across the plains following the Civil War suggested that western railroads would soon become a promising industry. General Palmer took his credentials to the Eastern Division of the Union Pacific, which was building a road across the plains of Kansas and which would soon adopt the optimistic name of Kansas Pacific. Palmer's first service with the Kansas Pacific gave him an opportunity to survey the land that his own railroad would be racing to reach a decade later. Originally, the Kansas Pacific was intended to connect with the Union Pacific's mainline near Fort Kearny, Nebraska; however, the urgings of the city fathers of the bustling, frontier town of Denver enticed the builders to head west for that city. In the fall of 1867, Palmer led survey parties across the thirty-second and thirty-fifth parallels in anticipation of a transcontinental line heading southwest from Denver across the Rio Grande Valley and on to the Pacific Ocean. Congress, however, did not share the enthusiasm of the Kansas Pacific's officials and refused to provide the necessary subsidy for the project.[2]

Meanwhile, the Kansas Pacific reached the "Queen City of the Plains" in the fall of 1870, and Palmer, who was now treasurer of the road, decided to leave the organization and strike out to pursue his own ambitions. Even before the Kansas Pacific reached Denver, Palmer had urged its directors to build west up the rich Arkansas Valley to Pueblo and then north along the one hundred mile stretch of the Front Range to Denver. When his advice went unheeded, the General moved to control this stretch for himself and envisioned a railroad running north and south along the entire base of the Rocky Mountains from Denver to El Paso; such a road would serve to tap the riches of the inner Rockies and would function as a feeder line between the major transcontinental railroads on their east to west axis. In the fall of 1870, Palmer was free to start building his dream.

The background for Palmer's next move had been laid the year before, when on a journey back East he had met a well-dressed, New York attorney by the name of William Proctor Mellen. Mellen had connections with eastern financiers and a prominent British financier, William Blackmore. The energetic Palmer needed these connections to provide capital for the pursuit of his dream. As Palmer was aspiring to be the railroad king of the Rockies, Mellen also had a daughter of interest to him. Nicknamed "Queen," nineteen-year-old Mary Lincoln Mellen was as desirable a catch as any bachelor of thirty-three could hope for, and by the following year Palmer had Mellen's financial backing and the hand of his daughter.[3] Not a bad start for a railroader who had yet to lay a mile of track.

On October 27, 1870, shortly after the Kansas Pacific arrived in Denver, the certificate of incorporation of the Denver and Rio Grande Railway Company was filed with the territorial legislature showing a capital stock of $2,500,000. The directorate for the first year was to consist of William P. Mellen of New York, R. Henry Lamborn of Philadelphia, Alexander Hunt of Denver, Howard J. Schuyler of Denver, and William Jackson Palmer of Colorado, who was designated as president. The certificate of incorporation listed one main line and seven branch lines to be established off of it. The announced route for the main line, the Denver and Rio Grande Railway, was south from Denver to the Arkansas River near Pueblo, westward through the "Big Canon of the Arkansas," south across Poncha Pass into the San Luis Valley to the Rio Grande River, and then along it to Santa Fe and El Paso. Once in El Paso the company intended to connect with the Mexican National Railway and operate on into Mexico City.[4]

While the Rio Grande's dreams for empire were large, the road soon became known as the "Baby Railroad," because unlike the major railroads that were driving west in 1870, Palmer decided to construct the Rio Grande in narrow gauge. Gauge in railroad terminology may be defined as the distance between the rails or the wheel span of the locomotive. Gauges varied throughout the United States until 1865 when Congress set the national standard at four feet, eight and one-half inches. Palmer chose the narrow gauge of three feet because it was more suited to the terrain he had to cross. Narrow gauge could climb steeper grades, turn tighter curves, and perhaps most important in Palmer's decision, it was less expensive to construct and maintain than the broad gauge.

As the tracks were laid south from Denver, Palmer planned the success of his line along three key points which were still important when the Rio Grande's rails came to Marshall Pass. First, he saw the road as the carrier of commerce from the mountains to the broad gauge lines in the east; not only were gold, silver, and other minerals important, but also coal, timber products, and agricultural produce would be transported on the narrow gauge. Second, the General acted as the forerunner of modern Chambers of Commerce and thought that the dry climate and beautiful scenery would induce tourists and health seekers to travel the Rio Grande. Lastly, Palmer saw the Rio Grande as the north-south connecting link between the transcontinental lines and the cities that were springing up along them. As time went on, these goals became reality, but not without bitter and bloody competition.

By 1878, Palmer had expanded south along the Front Range of the Rockies to El Moro, which is just north of the present-day Colorado-New Mexico border and Raton Pass, and across La Veta Pass to Alamosa in the San Luis Valley. A year later steps were taken to expand westward through the Royal Gorge, the deepest portion of the Big Canon of the Arkansas, from Cañon City, which had been reached in 1874.

By now Palmer's virtual monopoly on the area around Pueblo and Colorado Springs was threatened by the arrival of the broad gauge Atchison, Topeka and Santa Fe in Pueblo early in 1876. Its very name suggested that it intended to tap the rich New Mexican trade which Palmer was hoping to capture with the Rio Grande's arrival in Santa Fe. A confrontation arose between the Rio Grande and the Santa Fe involving armed conflicts at the two strategic points of Raton Pass and the Royal Gorge and a series of legal battles, which at one time had the Rio Grande under Santa Fe receivership.

After several years of bitter controversy, which saw the Santa Fe win the right of way to Raton Pass and the Rio Grande win the right of way through the Royal Gorge, the two companies reached an agreement in the Treaty of Boston. Formalized on March 27, 1880, it stated that the Denver and Rio Grande was prohibited from expanding south from its railhead at Española, New Mexico, or from crossing Raton Pass for a period of ten years, while the Atchison, Topeka, and Santa Fe was prohibited from expanding farther west from Cañon City at the mouth of the Royal Gorge for a period of ten years.[5]

At midnight on April 4, 1880,[6] the Rio Grande was released from Santa Fe receivership and Palmer made desperate plans to build west through the Royal Gorge. While Palmer never gave up the idea of a north to south line, the Rockies and their booming mining camps had acted as a magnet and pulled the axis of his line to the west. Soon it would be Salt Lake City that cheered the advances of the Rio Grande instead of Santa Fe. During the period the Denver and Rio Grande was under the management of the Santa Fe, the eastern road had laid about twenty-three miles of track west from Cañon City and had graded most of the roadbed along the remaining one hundred miles to the booming silver center of Leadville. By the compromise between the two companies the Rio Grande purchased this right of way and consequently made excellent time in getting to Leadville, arriving there in late July of 1880.[7]

As Palmer's railroad drew new life from the revenues of the Leadville trade, it was confronted with a new threat. Few historians will argue that the railroad history of the Colorado Rockies after 1880 shows the Denver and Rio Grande to have been the biggest, the toughest, and the best. Yet in 1880, its plans were influenced by a railroad that would be remembered not because of its corporate austerity, but because of its charisma which attracted the attention of the world.

No railroad emphasized the close ties of the Colorado narrow gauges to the land they served more completely than did the Denver, South Park, and Pacific. Originally organized in 1872 as the Denver, Georgetown, and Utah Railroad Company, the road went southwest out of Denver across South Park with the characteristic goal of eventually the Pacific. In the summer of 1880, the South Park had come out of the park of its name and crossed Trout Creek Pass into the valley of the Arkansas River, along which the Rio Grande's tracks ran north to Leadville. Plans called for the extension of the line up Chalk Creek into the heart of the Sawatch Range and over Altman Pass into the Gunnison country. In October of 1879, John Evans, the South Park's president, negotiated a joint operating agreement with Palmer concerning the proposed route. The agreement permitted Denver and Rio Grande trains to operate over South Park trackage into the Gunnison country in return for some concessions in the Leadville trade.[8]

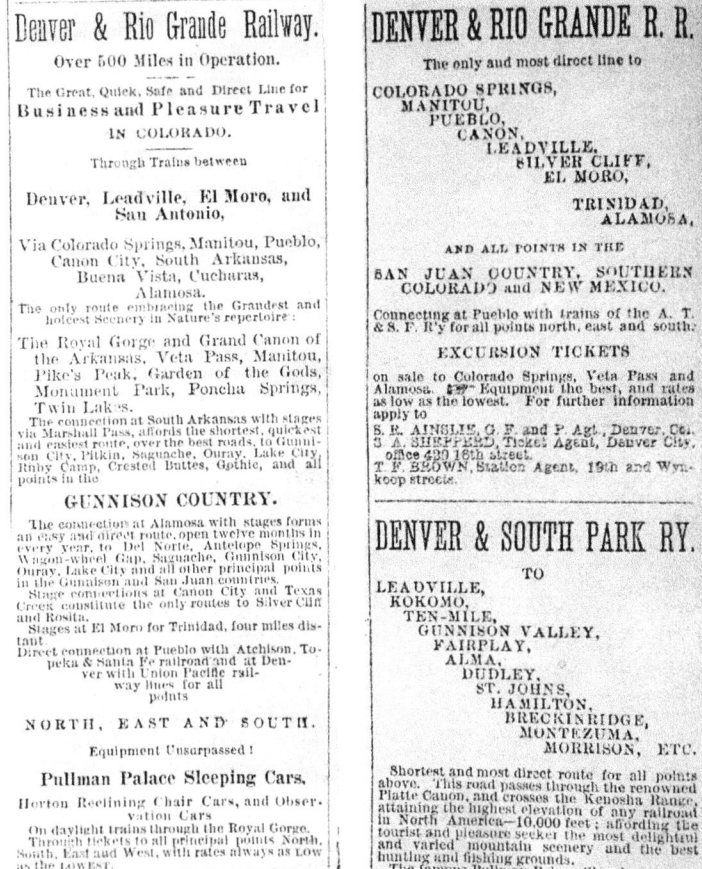

Left: Gunnison Review, *November 27, 1880.*
BOTH, DOW HELMERS COLLECTION

This arrangement seemed compatible with both parties until Evans sold the South Park to the eastern financial manipulator Jay Gould for $2,590,000 in November of 1880.[9] While the South Park under Evans's control was an agreeable partner with the Rio Grande, Gould ownership of the route threatened to link the South Park to Gould's giant Union Pacific and provide stiff competition for the Rio Grande. Palmer saw the move as a violation of the Boston Treaty to which the Union Pacific had been a third party in promising not to build into the central Colorado Rockies. In return, Palmer violated the joint operating agreement with the South Park.[10] When John Evans objected strongly to Palmer's intention of building a competing line to Gunnison, Palmer replied that the agreement had been made personally with Evans in his role as owner of the South Park and that it was not transferable to Gould. While he trusted Evans, Palmer had no intention of being left out of Gunnison

*A track gang takes a rest from throwing dirt and rock ballast on freshly laid track west of Shirley. This was June of 1881 and construction was going full speed in an attempt to reach Gunnison by August 1. Note the work train with an engine on each end in the background.*
WILLIAM H. JACKSON PHOTO; CHARLES LEAMING TUTT LIBRARY; DOW HELMERS COLLECTION

by trusting the "buccaneering maneuvers of the man who had wrecked the Erie,"[11] a comment referring to Gould's previous railroad dealings.

Now the race was on and the Gunnison country watched eagerly to see whether Denver, South Park, and Pacific or Denver and Rio Grande would be lettered on the first locomotive into the valley. What lay across the passes of the Continental Divide, Marshall, Altman, Monarch, and others, to interest the railroads? First it might be asked what real needs for a railroad in the Gunnison country lay beneath the urgings of civic leaders bent on community boosterism.

The Gunnison country, by definition the area drained by the Gunnison River before it emerges from the Black Canyon, is bounded on three sides by mountains—the Elk Range to the north, the Sawatch Range and the Continental Divide to the east, and the San Juan Mountains to the south. To the west, accessibility is hindered by the Black Canyon and several high mesas. Thus, despite the mineral and agricultural wealth of the valley, the towns in the area had to overcome their geographic isolation if their products were to reach the markets of the East. Cochetopa Pass, Marshall Pass, and the passes of the Taylor Park region offered routes to the railroads in the Arkansas Valley, but, as emphasized, wagon traffic over the passes was slow and hazardous. Railroads, once constructed over the obstacles, became a cheaper and faster means of transporting large quantities of materials in and out of the region. As the railroads pushed west, their routes played a major role in dictating which centers thrived and which became ghost towns.

Of course the railroads needed more incentives than "help-our-town-grow" editorials before they laid track, and the Gunnison country was rich in its offerings to the Rio Grande and the South Park. First, the Gunnison country was rich in minerals. The mines which made

Gunnison City a supply center and receiving point of goods coming into the country over the Marshall Pass Toll Road and other routes also demanded an economical outlet for the ores to be shipped out of the country. Not only were gold and silver important, but to the north of Gunnison the coal mines of Crested Butte offered to yield the best anthracite coal west of Pennsylvania, a product of special interest to a railroad whose source of locomotive power was coal.

Next there was the consideration of a transcontinental line west to Salt Lake City. True, there was the obstacle of the Black Canyon to overcome, but if this challenge could be met, a railroad connection between Denver and Salt Lake City through Colorado could be made. The mountains west of Denver severely hampered early attempts to push a line directly west from that city and in 1880 the route west from Salida through the Gunnison country looked promising. Lastly, the mineral wealth of the San Juans was open to the railroad that could gain access to its northern door. Already Otto Mears was constructing numerous toll roads throughout the San Juans which would one day accommodate railroad lines.

Indeed, the prize of the Gunnison country was inviting and it is doubtful that Palmer could have kept his hands off of it regardless of the joint agreement with John Evans. In his annual report of 1880, Palmer emphasized the importance of the outcome of the Royal Gorge fight in terms of the Gunnison country. "The contest for the Grand Canyon [Royal Gorge] was in reality a fight for the gateway, not to Leadville only, but to the far more important, because infinitely larger, mineral fields of the Gunnison country, the Blue and Eagle Rivers and Utah."[12] The key to the Western Slope did lie through the mountains west of the Rio Grande's town of Salida and both the Rio Grande and South Park realized it.

*This incomparable Jackson photograph depicts six levels of trackage and toll road on the west side of Marshall Pass. The summit of the pass is to the right. Rolling terrain allowed the right-of-way to be built with very little bridging and no tunnel.*

WILLIAM H. JACKSON PHOTO: COLORADO HISTORICAL SOCIETY: DOW HELMERS COLLECTION

*Photographer Jackson's great picture was sketched for Ingersoll's Crest of the Continent with some alterations. A bridge was added on on upper level and the original freight was transformed into a passenger train.*
DOW HELMERS COLLECTION

Railroad fever hit Gunnison as early as May of 1880 when a petition for a Denver and Rio Grande extension was circulated around town and signed by "all" county and city officials as well as some prominent citizens. In reporting the event the *Gunnison News* had the optimism to predict that the road would be in Gunnison by September 1 and that Gunnison would then be blessed with two railroads.[13] Little did the *News* know that the second railroad they were counting on, the South Park, was in for trouble. Railroad talk increased and on July 20 the *Rocky Mountain News* reported that George H. Owens, the general agent for J. L. Sanderson and Company, had received orders to sell through tickets, Denver to Gunnison, by the Rio Grande and Sanderson stages. The trip took twenty-three hours, leaving Denver on the overnight train and arriving in Gunnison the following evening. Cost for the one-way trip was $22.50.[14] As traffic swarmed over Marshall Pass during that summer, Sanderson charged ten to eleven dollars for a passage from Salida to Gunnison and did a land office business as they boasted "let the railroad come."[15]

Now the railroad was coming! Throughout the summer of 1880 survey teams under the supervision of Robert F. Weitbrec, a close friend of Palmer's and the construction manager of the Denver and Rio Grande, worked over Marshall Pass along Otto Mears's toll road and over Monarch Pass on the Continental Divide some fifteen miles to the north. By late August the *Gunnison News* speculated that the probable route would be from Salida to Poncha Springs and then over Marshall Pass with an 800-foot tunnel.[16] While the *News* guessed correctly that Marshall Pass and not Monarch would be used, the question provided some good betting and speculations on both sides of the Divide.

To the modern traveler who has crossed both Monarch and Marshall Passes, Marshall Pass would seem to be the obvious choice because of a more gentle grade. Indeed, this is true today in comparing the railroad grade of Marshall Pass to the highway grade of Monarch Pass, but strangely enough, the surveys which Weitbrec conducted during the summer of 1880 showed the two passes to be remarkably similar. Based on estimates by James McMurtrie, the chief engineer, the distance from Salida to Gunnison over Monarch Pass would be eighty-six and one-half miles while over Marshall Pass would be eighty-seven miles. Costs, which included grading and bridge construction, would run $1,133,250 over Monarch Pass and $1,223,750 over Marshall Pass.[17]

Two key issues were involved in the final decision of choosing Marshall Pass. First, while McMurtrie's estimates for Monarch showed its maximum grade to be 211 feet per mile, the same as on Marshall Pass, the canyons that run off Monarch's crest are much deeper and steeper than those on Marshall and the road would have had more difficulty snaking its way up than on the more rolling slopes of Marshall Pass. The decisive reason, however, rested with Otto Mears. Throughout the summer the wagons and stages had done a reasonable job of smoothing his toll road over Marshall Pass. Now in the fall of 1880, a competitive road was being built over Monarch Pass and he was busy building new roads into the heart of the San Juans and carrying on negotiations with the Utes. Realizing that the railroad would severely cut in to his profits, Mears agreed through Weitbrec to sell the toll road to the Rio

*This William Henry Jackson photo was taken in the summer of 1881 prior to the construction of the summit snowsheds and before the track had even been adequately ballasted. The view looks northeast through the summit cut to Mount Ouray.*
WILLIAM H. JACKSON PHOTO; CHARLES LEAMING TUTT LIBRARY; DOW HELMERS COLLECTION

Grande for $13,000.[18] Thus, with the major portion of the route to Gunnison already graded, the Denver and Rio Grande could hope to make faster time and beat the South Park to Gunnison.

In the middle of September, the first concrete step in building the Gunnison branch was taken when the Rio Grande began driving piles for a bridge across the Arkansas River at Salida.[19] Two weeks later, although still reluctant to name a definite route over the Divide, the *Mountain Mail* quoted Rio Grande General Manager D. C. Dodge as predicting that within a week some 500 men would be at work on the branch. Already the grading was done between Salida and Poncha Springs five miles to the west and the grade was being readied for rails and ties.[20] Construction leaped forward in a desperate drive to get as far as possible before the winter weather set in. By late October the bridge across the Arkansas at Salida was completed,[21] and on November 14, 1880, the five miles of track to Poncha Springs were opened. Service started to Poncha Springs on November 22 with connecting Sanderson stages to the Gunnison country.

As crews graded south out of Poncha Springs toward the base of Marshall Pass and the start of the toll road, the Rio Grande was again aided by a stroke of luck. During the railroad war of the late 1870s, the Santa Fe had done some advance grading for a line into the San Luis Valley over Poncha Pass and some of the work was incorporated into the Rio Grande line, saving much time. By now winter was descending in full force. The temperature dropped to twenty-three degrees below zero at Salida on November 18 and many of the laborers quit. Although some stayed on and work continued through the winter, the close of 1880 found activity slowed as the Denver and Rio Grande waited for a hint of spring.[22]

As the Rio Grande graded toward Marshall Pass, what had become of the railroad which the *Gunnison News* had spoken so confidently of having even before Palmer's line? December of 1880 found the Denver, South Park, and Pacific at St. Elmo on Chalk Creek about fifteen miles west of Palmer's road up the Arkansas River. Like the Rio Grande, it had been slowed by bad weather, but the real reason the little road, which at one time held the lead in the race, was falling behind was an epic project which would soon capture the imagination of railroad buffs around the world. Rather than battle the heights and bad weather of 12,124-foot Altman Pass, the South Park decided to bore through the Continental Divide at the 11,500-foot level, thus giving birth to the Alpine Tunnel.

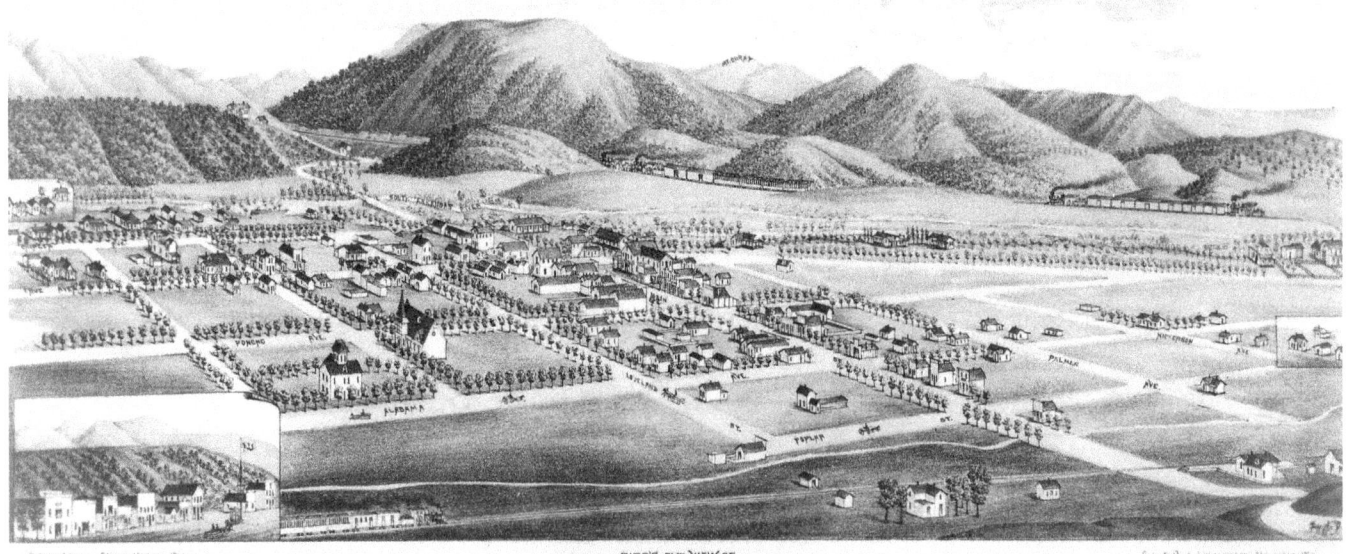

BIRD'S EYE VIEW OF
**PONCHO, COLO.**
1882.
6900 FT. ABOVE SEA LEVEL.

1. Post Office, H. H. Fulton, Post-Master.
2. Poncho Herald, W. C. & F. M. Tompkins, Editor and Prop's.
3. D. & R. G. R. R. Depot.
4. Poncho Hot Springs Hotel and Bath Rooms.
5. Meat Market, Wm. Appleby, Prop'r

A—School House.
B—Free Reading Room.
C—Presbyterian Church
D—American House, J. L. Royer, Prop'r.
E—Poncho Spring House, H. A. Jackson, Prop'r.
F—Restaurant, Mrs. Maggie Fleck, Proprietress

*The San Luis branch cross-over, just above Mears Junction, east side of Marshall Pass. Train on lower track has just descended from Marshall Pass. Train on trestle is arriving from Villa Grove, via Poncha Pass and will loop to the right and join the Marshall Pass mainline and both trains will proceed to Poncha Junction and Salida.*
WILLIAM H. JACKSON PHOTO; DENVER PUBLIC LIBRARY - WESTERN HISTORY DEPARTMENT;
DOW HELMERS COLLECTION

James A. Evans, the chief engineer of the project, had assumed in planning the Alpine Tunnel that the mountain was solid rock. Once the drilling started it was found that it was ninety-five percent decomposed granite and loose stone and was saturated with running water. Consequently, a large additional sum had to be spent on twelve by-twelve California redwood for timbering. When completed, the tunnel was 1,772 feet long, twelve feet wide and seventeen feet high. Some idea of the weather conditions on the Continental Divide can be gauged by the fact that there was no need for a ventilating system in the tunnel because the wind blew it clean after each passing locomotive. After six hundred and ninety-nine days of drilling, the Alpine Tunnel was holed through on December 21, 1881. Nine more months would pass before the South Park finally reached Gunnison.[23] The Alpine Tunnel reserved a spot in railroad lore for the South Park but it cost dearly in construction costs, a year's delay in reaching the Gunnison country, and in lives and materials as the years went by.

While the Denver, South Park, and Pacific would be more than a year behind the Rio Grande in entering Gunnison because of the Alpine Tunnel, Palmer was not taking any chances as 1881 dawned. Although it had been evident for some time, the axis of the line that once dreamed of reaching Mexico City was now committed to seek its survival in tapping the veins of east to west commerce. Palmer's foresight and crafty planning probably called for a through line to Salt Lake City over Marshall Pass and across the Gunnison country long before a Rio Grande survey team worked its way into Gunnison City on January 8, 1881, and announced that they were surveying a transcontinental line to Utah. This was the first direct indication to citizens of Gunnison that they would be on a transcontinental line and that the route over Marshall Pass would be more than just a branch line into the Gunnison country.

During the first week of February, work began in earnest at grading and laying track from Poncha Springs six miles south to Owens Sawmill. By the middle of the month more than 1,100 men and 150 teams were at work battling cold and snow as they set the ties and spiked down the rails on the frozen ground. At Owens Sawmill the railroad negotiated for land from a Mr. Owens to build a depot, which would soon become known as Mears, named after the man whose toll road ran over nearby Marshall Pass. Within the year Mears became Mears Junction as the Rio Grande ran another spur south over Poncha Pass and down the San Luis Valley to their line at Alamosa. While Salida was destined to become an important railroad center, the hustle and bustle of the railhead was now at Poncha Springs and would soon leapfrog over the pass until the road reached Gunnison.[24]

On February 19, 1881, the *Mountain Mail* reported that it was not certain where the next terminal point on the pass would be. Speculation had it that the railroad would either halt at Mears or at the mouth of Silver Creek two and one half miles up the valley to catch its breath.[25] From the standpoint of a railroad racing for business there was no time to stop and catch its breath; time was of the essence. Naturally there were things which interrupted and slowed the tracklayers' efficiency. As pointed out, one was the bitter and unpredictable weather. The other, of even greater concern, was the difficulty in obtaining dependable workers. Workers would sign on, stay a few weeks, and then when the weather turned bad or they got the urge to move they would simply pick up and be gone. In a report dated March 16, 1881, Robert Weitbrec, still manager of construction, reported that "the most serious difficulty we have had to encounter has been and is still the securing of a sufficient quantity of good labor." Weitbrec went on to say that the highest wages ever paid to railroad laborers in Colorado were being paid by the Rio Grande but still it was difficult to retain a complete working force. Weitbrec's

*A construction train on drawbar of engine No. 83, pauses on the crossover above Mears Junction as it returns to Poncha Junction from the San Luis branch. Marshall Pass mainline below.*
WILLIAM H. JACKSON PHOTO; DENVER PUBLIC LIBRARY - WESTERN HISTORY DEPARTMENT;
DOW HELMERS COLLECTION

*Shirley, Colorado, located thirteen miles from Salida and two miles west of Mears, saw great activity while the D&RG was building over Marshall Pass. The depot and water tank are at right of photo. Two cars, including a passenger coach are on track 15-A, which ran to the Rawley Mine and Mill in lower Silver Creek. The great loop is less than a mile upgrade from Shirley.*   RICHARD A. RONZIO, DOW HELMERS COLLECTION

following comments applied to the entire Denver and Rio Grande system, but Marshall Pass shared them:

> *Since November, 1879, there have been an average of at least 1,000 laborers per month shipped from Denver and Pueblo to the various grading camps.*
>
> *In addition to this our Company had advanced the fares of 200 men brought from Canada, 250 from St. Louis, 300 from Chicago, 1,000 from Kansas, the laborers in each case agreeing to refund the amount when earned in our service.*
>
> *In nearly all cases the men deserted, many to the mines, a few returned to their homes, and the Lord probably knows where the rest are.*[26]

Weitbrec reported that the Rio Grande had spent $41,350 in fares for these men and that out of that only $8,000 had been repaid. Clearly, the experience demonstrated that such a recruitment plan for labor resulted in the majority of cases to attract only riff-raff who were only interested in a free ride to Colorado. After that Weitbrec decided that if a man could not raise enough money to get to the grading camps, he would not be worth much.[27]

Despite labor troubles, work continued on the Gunnison Branch with the rails reaching Mears Junction on March 26, 1881.[28] The following day trains began running to Mears which became a temporary freight and passenger terminus. Within a week the rails were laid to Silver Creek and it became the railhead for passengers and freight as the tracklayers wound their way up the pass. Silver Creek was located at the junction of Silver Creek and Poncha Creek and like so many early towns soon had its name changed; it became Shirley. At Shirley the serious

*A freight train negotiates the long curve above Shirley shortly after construction.*
COLORADO HISTORICAL SOCIETY

climbing began for the attack on the pass which lay twelve railroad grade miles away and 2200 vertical feet higher. By the middle of April, Shirley was a booming construction camp boasting fourteen large business tents, eight of them saloons and dance halls. Track laying for the moment had ceased because of a shortage of rails and while the grading continued, Shirley enjoyed the overnight prosperity of being a railhead.[29]

It is interesting to note in the newspaper accounts of this era that as the railroad got farther west of Salida the references to the route in the *Mountain Mail* became fewer. While Salida had the consolation of becoming a key railroad center, they were obviously envious of the fact that Gunnison would soon be the railhead for the wealth of the Gunnison country and the San Juans. As Gunnison eagerly looked forward to this event, the *Gunnison Review* reported early in April that large crews were at work on the pass and were "making the dirt fly." The tunnel that the *Review* had speculated on the previous fall would not be needed. A fifty-foot deep cut was blasted through the hog back ridge on the summit of the pass where William Marshall had huddled seven years before.

In a deviation from their frenzied community boosterism, the *Review* went on to report that the toll road over Marshall Pass was in very poor shape. Spring thaws had caused snow and mud slides making it "impossible to get wagons through." In addition to the spring thaws which made the road a sea of mud, the Denver and Rio Grande was making no effort to keep up the toll road they now owned when they were busy building a railroad which soon would replace it.[30] Although the *Review* lamented about the freight that had to detour around Marshall Pass and come into Gunnison via Cochetopa Pass, an article the following week suggested that the condition of the road had improved considerably. As witnessed by Carrie Strahorn's adventures, a Sanderson stage journey over the pass was not the safest or easiest undertaking known to the western traveler, but nevertheless, on Thursday, April 7, three loads of

*Construction crews and trains occupy the sidings at Grays during the building of the route. In accepted practice near the "front," the #401 is headed up grade at one end of the train while an unidentified engine is headed down grade at the other.*
DENVER PUBLIC LIBRARY - WESTERN HISTORY DEPARTMENT

Sanderson coaches crowded with passengers braved the ride over Marshall Pass and arrived in Gunnison in one piece.[31]

As late as April, Gunnison folks seemed to have no conception of the problems at Alpine Tunnel and were still optimistically speculating that both the Rio Grande and South Park would be in Gunnison by the first of August at the latest.[32] As Gunnison cheered, the railhead remained at Shirley. Stage traffic was so heavy that many people were forced to lay over a day at the town. By the middle of May the town could boast seventy-five tents and buildings. Among them, the *Gunnison Review* asserted, were four forwarding houses, five groceries, two clothing stores, two hotels, one drug store, three bakeries, two meat markets, two blacksmith shops, one wholesale liquor store, two butter and egg depots, and restaurants and saloons without number. Undoubtedly, someone would soon be screaming that here indeed was the next capital of Colorado. But the railroad was moving on. On May 28 Green and Foody, the construction company which had the contract for laying the rails, commenced laying steel west from Shirley. For Shirley this meant its days were numbered.[33]

*"Pretty as a picture" is this handsome little 200 series narrow gauge locomotive, running light downgrade, after helping a train up Marshall Pass. It slides effortlessly over the great trestle bridging Ouray Creek, between Marshall Pass and Pocono, about three miles downgrade on the east side.*
FRANCIS AND FREDA RIZZARI; DOW HELMERS COLLECTION

On June 21, 1881, as the Sanderson coach pulled into Gunnison, the weary passengers announced that theirs had been the first passenger train to arrive at the summit of Marshall Pass. From Shirley to the summit the scenery was sensational and to the passengers' surprise the ride had been smooth and easy. The *Gunnison News-Democrat* went on to say:

> *And this is not the best of the news. It is positively stated by those in authority that the terminus of the Gunnison branch will be at Sargents (at the foot of Marshall Pass on the west) by the Fourth of July. From Sargents to Gunnison as everybody knows is a comparatively level county, and as the larger part of the road from that point to this has*

*been already graded, there is little doubt but that the whistle of the first locomotive in this valley will serenade the people of Gunnison by the first of August.*[34]

The curves and the roundabout route of the road as it wound its way down the west side of the pass were such that this report proved, as so many others were, to be overly optimistic. Nevertheless, while the Fourth of July found the Rio Grande still several miles above Sargent (while called Sargents today, it always appeared on railroad timetables as "Sargent.") the citizens of Salida organized the first of many excursion specials on the Gunnison line.

At 6:20 A. M. on the morning of the Fourth a party of twenty-five adults and children took the morning train out of Salida for the summit of Marshall Pass. At Shirley the train was turned and backed up the pass as many of the excursionists stood on the end platform of the last car as it was pushed up the grade. On the 10,846-foot summit the party-goers engaged in a snow-ball fight and before long had to build a fire to keep warm. As is so customary along the Continental Divide during July and August an afternoon shower swept in off the slopes of Mount Ouray, but failed to dampen the celebration. After the excursionists hurried to the shelter of the coaches, the train was backed down the west side of the pass four or five miles along the windings and twistings of the terraced slope. They finally returned to Salida in an evening storm. The *Mountain Mail* remarked, somewhat tongue-in-cheek, that some of the passengers got wet although it didn't seem to hurt them "as they sometimes use water."[35]

The history of Marshall Pass proved to be a history of extremes. Excursionists and tourists would stare in awe at the scenery and engineering marvels of the line one day but the next day

*An eastbound freight and a westbound Gunnison excursion train pause in the summit cut of Marshall Pass on August 28, 1881, before the construction of the summit snowsheds. Note the additional helper engines behind the locomotive of the passenger train.*

DENVER PUBLIC LIBRARY - WESTERN HISTORY DEPARTMENT

*Snowsheds were built rapidly during the fall of 1881 in an effort to stem the fury of Colorado winters. This shed and unfinished siding are close to the summit on the eastern side.*

DENVER PUBLIC LIBRARY - WESTERN HISTORY DEPARTMENT; DOW HELMERS COLLECTION

would bring horrible rail accidents. On July 6, the Gunnison extension recorded its first rail fatality when a train ran over a man near Poncha Springs. Railroading in those days was a dangerous business and the body of the man was so badly mangled that no one could identify the unfortunate victim.[36]

By the time rails were being laid down the west side of Marshall Pass, Gunnison had become quite excited over the exact location of the Denver and Rio Grande depot. Originally one townsite, the town had split during the winter of 1879-80 into the two rival towns of East and West Gunnison. The dissident faction of the new town of West Gunnison then made a deal with the South Park to locate its depot in their section of the town. Soon it became apparent that the Rio Grande also intended to locate its depot in the western section of town. Naturally this caused a great deal of rivalry between the two sections.

*A powerful little 30 series, Baldwin-built engine, backs away, having unloaded lumber for snowsheds at Marshall Pass summit.*
F. A. NIM PHOTO: DENVER PUBLIC LIBRARY - WESTERN HISTORY DEPARTMENT; DOW HELMERS COLLECTION

This provides a point of digression to discuss the policies of the Rio Grande in regard to townsites. General Palmer's empire was not limited to railroads. He had founded Colorado Springs when the railroad started south from Denver and started a policy of land speculation to help pay for his road. His system was to buy land along the right of way and then when he came to a town that was screaming for a railroad he would build his own town with a railroad station within a few miles of the existing site. This created a magnetic force to his own townsite because of the railroad connection and in turn the Rio Grande received the profits from the sale of land in the townsite. This was the way that South Pueblo was established and why Salida is recognized today while the name Cleora has long since been forgotten. The threat of the South Park arriving in

*This William Henry Jackson photo looks south on the west side to a construction camp during the hectic days of the summer of 1881.*
WILLIAM H. JACKSON PHOTO; COLORADO HISTORICAL SOCIETY

*William H. Jackson brought his bulky cameras to Marshall Pass during construction days. Here, workmen construct the vast snowsheds over the apex of Marshall Pass.*
WILLIAM H. JACKSON PHOTO; CHARLES LEAMING TUTT LIBRARY;
DOW HELMERS COLLECTION

*During the construction rush of 1881, Marshall Pass was dotted with tent cities for the workers. The rails have not yet reached this camp on the west side of the pass and its inhabitants were working on grading the roadbed.*
DENVER PUBLIC LIBRARY - WESTERN HISTORY DEPARTMENT

Gunnison prohibited Palmer from such high-handed speculation in the Gunnison country, but the Denver and Rio Grande did become one-third owner of the West Gunnison Town and Land Company. The new townsite was close enough to old Gunnison that the older town did not die. While antagonisms were deep for many years, the rival sections have since become one again.

On the afternoon of July 16, the first regular passenger service from Salida rolled into Sargent. Although travel on the roadbed was slow to allow the track time to settle and adjust, freight service was started two days later and soon Sargent was enjoying the boom of being a railhead. As Shirley slipped quietly into the role of a peaceful, little railroad siding, the *Gunnison Review* spoke in glowing terms of the boom in Sargent that Shirley had experienced just three months before. The *Review* noted in the middle of July that probably fifty businesses were doing business there, most of them occupying tents. One man had been killed already in the roaring action and merchants took advantage of the boom that was certain to end abruptly with the Rio Grande's arrival in Gunnison.

In the boom year of 1881 the Rio Grande was pushing west on several fronts. During that year the famous comment that the Denver and Rio Grande had more men working for it than the United States Army was attributed to Alexander Hunt by the *Denver Tribune*. Of the 32,000

## II | The Coming of the Rails

men Hunt cited, however, 19,000 were employed on the Palmer line in Mexico, 4,000 were at work in New Mexico, 6,000 in Colorado, and the remainder in Utah.[37] Nevertheless, as has been seen, Construction Boss Weitbrec had his problems with the labor forces and among them were disputes with workers who did stay.

Just as the Rio Grande was entering Sargent, five tie cutters on the western slope of Marshall Pass attempted to wreck a train to show their disagreement with the railroad. The tie cutters were paid by the tie and when a locomotive spewing hot cinders chugged by and set a freshly cut stack on fire they demanded payment. While the railroad did not refuse to make reparations, they were at least slow in making payment. Assuming that they were not to be paid, the tie cutters hired two teen-age boys for a dollar each to wreck a train. On Saturday, July 16, Jacob and James Cross, one sixteen and the other thirteen, went to work with an advance of twenty-five cents each. On a steep grade on the western slope, the boys first greased a section of track and then piled spikes and a telegraph pole on the track. A westbound train coming downgrade managed to stop just in front of the barrier. Rio Grande officials were notified of the attempt and by 3:00 P.M. the boys had been captured and had readily confessed. The railroad went on to capture the five men who had paid for the venture, and the boys, each out seventy-five cents of expected income, went to Shirley as witnesses against them.[38]

While the Rio Grande was busy chasing train wreckers, the city fathers of Gunnison were busy planning a reception for the railroad. On July 29, when the railroad was almost to Parlin, twelve miles east of Gunnison, the citizens held a meeting to discuss plans for a celebration

*Engine 227, a 2-8-0 built by Grant, drifts below Shawano with five "high" revenue cars and a caboose. Much timber had been cut to clear the right-of-way. Work gangs had not yet ballasted the track.*
WILLIAM H. JACKSON PHOTO; COLORADO HISTORICAL SOCIETY; DOW HELMERS COLLECTION

when the railroad arrived. The sentiment ranged from a Mr. Levi's proposal to appoint a committee of five to collect donations for a hearty welcome celebration to Judge Smith's observation that when he rode the rails he would have to pay so why should he donate money for the railroad's account. Finally, after an eloquent plea emphasizing the importance of the railroad in the best terms of community boosterism, it was decided to welcome the railroad's arrival with a celebration. So as not to slight the South Park, it was then decided to welcome both the Rio Grande and the South Park with celebrations.

A few days later the first of many unfortunate accidents occurred on the summit of Marshall Pass. Gordon Chappell described the event in the *Colorado Rail Annual*:

> *On August 3 an unfortunate accident occurred at the top of the pass, where the westbound passenger train had paused at the summit. A freight climbing up from Shirley with the throttle wide open ran into the rear car of the passenger train before the engineer could shut off steam, and the jolt pushed the passenger train down the 4 per cent grade on the western slope. Before the startled passenger engineer could halt his train it ran into a construction train that was being switched onto a siding to allow the passenger train to pass. The collision derailed several cars and it was two hours before the line was clear and the passenger train could continue.*[39]

There were no fatalities, but in the initial collision a woman either jumped or was thrown through a window and suffered some bruises and internal injuries.[40]

August 3 was also the day that Charles Groff, the Denver and Rio Grande's Gunnison agent, and General Freight Agent Eccles arrived in town. They had come from the railhead six miles east of town and reported that a mile and three-quarters of track had been laid that afternoon. Agent Eccles assumed the usual public relations role for the Rio Grande and assured Gunnison residents that there was no reason in the world why Gunnison should not replace Denver and Pueblo as the supply point for the mountain country west of the Divide. It was the railroad's contention, he asserted, to give the Gunnison country low rates to encourage shipping and business. Indeed, he had the speech well prepared from the many previous times he had spoken in the same vein at every other town the Rio Grande had passed through. Gunnison provided one more opportunity to practice along the route to Salt Lake City.[41]

Two days later, on the evening of August 5, citizens on the corner of Main Street and Tomichi Avenue in downtown Gunnison heard the long, moaning wail of a locomotive echo down the valley of the Tomichi for the first time. Looking east the group could see a little diamond stacked engine belching black smoke and slowly nosing its way around the bluff near J. H. Haverly's ranch about a mile to the east. Swarms of workmen worked by lantern light into the night on the remaining grade into the city.

The next morning work continued and at 2:25 P. M. on Saturday, August 6, 1881, the rails of the Denver and Rio Grande Railway were spiked down across Main Street, completing the line from Salida to Gunnison over Marshall Pass which would continue for three-quarters of a century. A few minutes later the first engine to reach Gunnison, named appropriately the "Pacific Slope," rolled out onto the freshly laid track. Behind the engine came an assorted collection of battered cars which housed many of the workmen of the line. Called the "hotel" by the railroaders, this home on rails had left Poncha Springs in March and slowly wound its way over the pass. Soon a supply train with rails, switches, ties, and spikes was pulled into town by the "Grand Cañon." The temperature was up in the nineties that day and many people missed the initial entry, but as the afternoon cooled a crowd began to gather to watch the track being laid on west from Main Street. A rumor spread that a passenger train would arrive that same day, but by 3:30 the supply train had been ordered back to Sargent taking away the possibility of another train being on the single track.

All day Sunday the workmen worked feverishly staking down sidings and switches for the spur up to the coal mines at Crested Butte. The next morning, August 8, a crowd of civic leaders and citizens gathered around the depot site to welcome the first passenger train into the Gunnison country. Pulled by the "Badito," the train consisted of two coal cars, baggage cars, and two coaches—the "Albuquerque" and the "Saguache," that had been assembled up in Sargent for the run to the railhead. Shortly before noon the first regularly scheduled passenger train east out of Gunnison departed for Marshall Pass and Salida. Later that afternoon the regular passenger train from Salida arrived. That evening a banquet was given by the City Council and the Gunnison Board of Trade (the early equivalent of a Chamber of Commerce) for the railroad officials who had come into town on an afternoon special. Flattery flowed thick as honey as townspeople toasted the railroad and vice versa to commemorate the inauguration of the beginning of sixty years of passenger service over Marshall Pass. The mountains had been matched and now the fight would begin to tame them. Ahead lay the years of tapping the rich potential of Colorado's mountains and placing the state in contact with the rest of a rapidly growing nation.

*In 1885 it was "The Scenic Line of America" but in this advertisement, published in the "Official Railway Guide" the little railroad had become "The Scenic Line of the World." A mention is made of eight trains daily between Pueblo and Denver.*
DOW HELMERS COLLECTION

[1] Robert E. Riegel, "Palmer, William Jackson," *The Dictionary of American Biography*, 1933 ed., XIV, p. 195.

[2] Robert G. Athearn, *Rebel of the Rockies* (New Haven: Yale University Press, 1962), pp. 3-4.

[3] *Ibid.*, p. 6.

[4] George L. Anderson, *General William J. Palmer, A Decade of Colorado Railroad Building, 1870-1880* (Colorado Springs: Colorado College Publications, 1936 ), pp. 54-55.

[5] Athearn, Rebel of the Rockies, pp. 95-96.

[6] *Ibid.*, p. 98.

[7] "Summary of Construction of Denver and Rio Grande Railroad to and within Gunnison Country," Denver and Rio Grande Archives, No. 3265 B.

[8] Gordon Chappell, "Scenic Line of the World," *The Colorado Rail Annual*, No. 8, 1970, p. 10.

[9] Sprague, *The Great Gates*, p. 272.

[10] Chappell, "Scenic Line of the World," p. 10.

[11] Sprague, *The Great Gates*, p. 273.

[12] Denver and Rio Grande Archives, 3265 B.

[13] *Gunnison News*, May 1, 1880, p. 3.

[14] *Rocky Mountain News*, July 20, 1880, p. 8.

[15] *Gunnison News*, August 28, 1880, p. 3.

[16] *Ibid.*, August 21, 1880, p. 3.

[17] Construction Records, Robert F. Weitbrec Collection, Colorado State Historical Society, File Folder 13, Notebook 6, pp. 111-12.

[18] Letter, H. P. Bennet to H. A. Risley, April 27, 1882, Denver and Rio Grande Archives, 4307.

[19] *Mountain Mail*, September 18, 1880, p. 3.

[20] *Ibid.*, October 2, 1880, p. 3.

[21] *Ibid.*, October 23, 1880, p. 3.

[22] Chappell, "Scenic Line of the World," pp. 15-16.

[23] Sprague, *The Great Gates*, pp. 271-72.

[24] Chappell, "Scenic Line of the World," p. 17.

[25] *Mountain Mail*, February 19, 1881, p. 3.

[26] Denver and Rio Grande Archives, 3265 B. p. 2.

[27] *Ibid.*, p. 3.

[28] *Mountain Mail*, March 26, 1881, p. 3.

[29] Chappell, "Scenic Line of the World," p. 19 .

[30] *Gunnison Review*, April 2, 1881, p. 2.

[31] *Gunnison Review*, April 9, 1881, p. 3 .

[32] *Ibid.*, April 16, 1881, p. 2.

[33] Chappell, "Scenic Line of the World," p. 22.

[34] *Gunnison News-Democrat*, June 25, 1881, p. 6.

[35] *Mountain Mail*, July 6, 1881, p. 3.

[36] Chappell, "Scenic Line of the World," p. 23.

[37] *Ibid.*, p. 27.

[38] *Gunnison Review*, July 23, 1881, p. 2.

[39] Chappell, "Scenic Line of the World," p. 28.

[40] *Mountain Mail*, August 6, 1881, p. 3.

[41] Chappell, "Scenic Line of the World," p. 31.

# III
# CORNERSTONE OF AN EMPIRE

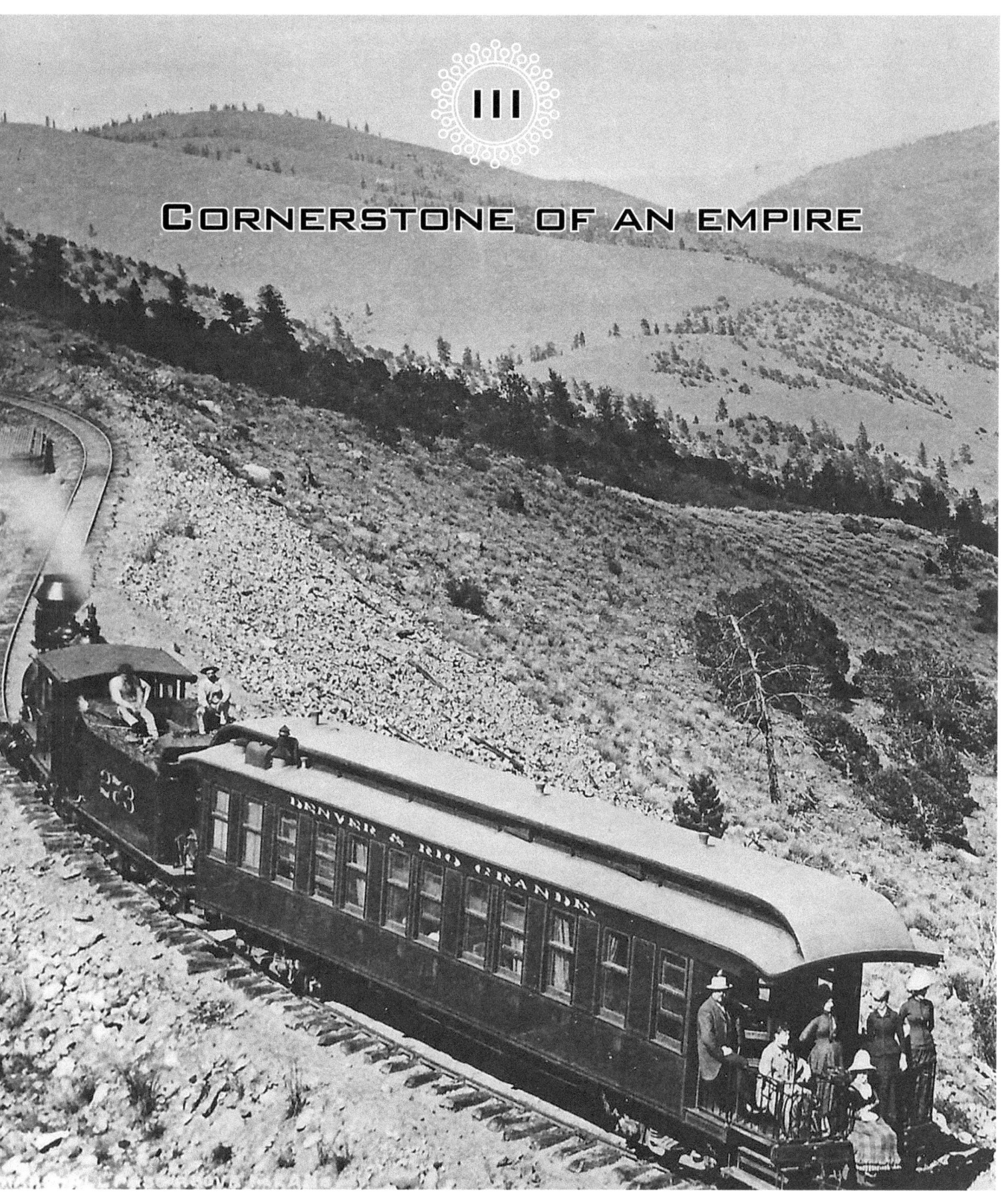

*Railroad officials and their ladies revel in the unmatched beauty of Marshall Pass in the springtime as Engine 273 slowly takes their coach with its spacious observation platform, upgrade on the east side of the pass.*
WILLIAM H. JACKSON PHOTO; DENVER PUBLIC LIBRARY - WESTERN HISTORY DEPARTMENT:
DOW HELMERS COLLECTION

## III
## CORNERSTONE OF AN EMPIRE

*Back to them thar hills, I went singing, one glad, glorious refrain,*
*The old Rio Grande following me on, with the faithful ore train.*
*I have mined on the highest mountain peaks, Massive, Aetna, and Ouray,*
*Never felt lost or alone, because the Rio Grande was not far away.*

Frank Gimlett
"The Hermit of Arbor Villa"

The coming of the railroads played an important role in the opening of the West and in deciding which of the numerous frontier towns would survive and which would become only memories. The arrival of the Denver and Rio Grande Railway in Gunnison soon fulfilled the reasons why General Palmer had decided to build over Marshall Pass in the first place. Gunnison was soon swamped by a rush of business flowing into town over Rio Grande tracks, and the railroad profited from the mineral wealth it carried out of the country. During August of 1881, freight receipts in Gunnison averaged an incredible $6,000 per day with more than 260 cars waiting to be unloaded on certain days.[1] The railroad yards were a picture of engines switching here and there moving empty cars out of the way and pushing full ones up to the platforms to be unloaded. No sooner were the tracks of the Rio Grande laid to Gunnison, than the tracklayers turned north toward the rich coal deposits at Crested Butte. Construction on the main line west was important, but the fall of 1881 found much of the Rio Grande work force building on the Crested Butte extension because it offered a ready source of revenue.

From Gunnison the main line ran west to connect the eastern slope with the riches of the San Juan Mountains. Branch lines off the Marshall Pass route were built into Lake City in 1889 and Ridgway in 1887 from the north. Rio Grande lines also reached into the mineral belt to Silverton in 1882 and South Fork in 1881. Palmer's last major consideration had been for a transcontinental route west, and he obtained a part of it by building west through portions of the Black Canyon, over Cerro Summit to Montrose and Grand Junction, and on to Salt Lake City. In March of 1883, the rails of the Denver and Rio Grande were joined with those of the Palmer affiliate, the Denver and Rio Grande Western Railway Company near Green River, Utah, completing a through line from Denver to Salt Lake City. The distance of the route was 735 miles and required thirty-five hours.[2] From Salt Lake City the Rio Grande could connect its traffic to the west along the Central Pacific. From 1881 until the completion of the Rio Grande broad gauge line over Tennessee Pass west of Leadville in 1890, Marshall Pass on the line through Gunnison was the mainstay of Palmer's transcontinental efforts. It was also the only transcontinental route through Colorado. The slopes of Marshall Pass had been tamed and now with its position as the cornerstone of the Rio Grande's transcontinental system secure, it made ready for its years of glory.

Throughout the fall of 1881, improvements were continually made on the roadbed over Marshall Pass as the track settled and shifted into a permanent position. In October, carpenters on the pass began work on a series of snowsheds, designed to protect the track on the upper reaches of the pass from the drifting and blowing snow. Despite these efforts, train service over Marshall Pass became erratic as winter became firmly entrenched on the Continental Divide. As early as November 13, snow interfered with train operations and passengers complained of being delayed while the snow was cleared. The *Gunnison Daily News-Democrat* admonished those who complained of having suffered from hunger during the delay by asserting that no person should attempt to cross the Divide during the winter without taking a full day's rations with him.[3]

On November 16, trainmaster J. C. Myers was in Gunnison telling the *News-Democrat* that a mile of snowsheds had been built on the pass and that the sheds would enable the railroad to keep the pass open all winter. Myers explained that the newspapers had greatly exaggerated the recent delays and that they had been caused by accidents and late trains from the east rather than by snow. Nevertheless, even as Myers spoke, Marshall Pass gave a prologue to what would become a common occurrence during the years the railroad operated over it. On November 16, the westbound passenger train was stranded at the summit by a snowstorm which blocked the line toward Gunnison and stranded three freights in three-foot deep snow. Before the line could be cleared, a second passenger train was brought to a halt by the storm.[4] The snowsheds helped keep the track clear, but they could not defeat the fury of a Colorado winter.

*Sweeping view of the final miles of railroad west of Marshall summit, with Mount Ouray in the background. Four levels of track are visible plus two segments of the wagon road built by Otto Mears.*
WILLIAM H. JACKSON PHOTO; DENVER PUBLIC LIBRARY - WESTERN HISTORY DEPARTMENT; DOW HELMERS COLLECTION

*Probably the greatest and most widely seen view of Marshall Pass was this William H. Jackson photo made in the 1880s. It shows the snowsheds on the west side, and the famous watch-tower. Hand-colored, this photo was reproduced on post cards by the H. H. Tammen Co.*
WILLIAM H. JACKSON PHOTO, COURTESY JACKSON C. THODE, DOW HELMERS COLLECTION

In addition to accidents and delays caused by the snow that first winter, the line was further clogged by a rush of men and materials heading west for work on the extension to Utah. On February 18, 1882, such congestion caused an accident on the summit of the pass. A westbound freight loaded with construction materials was cut into three sections for the trip over the pass. The first section stopped to switch in the dark of the nine-hundred foot, double-tracked, summit snowshed. A westbound passenger train successfully passed the second and third sections of the freight and was in the process of passing a work train in the double-tracked snowshed when the engineer saw the lights of the first section of the freight. Despite his whistle of "down brakes" and throwing the engine into reverse, the passenger train plowed into the caboose of the freight. Most critically injured was the conductor of the freight, Frank Seeley, who had been climbing from the caboose to the boxcar ahead of it and had his legs smashed by the roof of the caboose. It was concluded that Seeley was at fault in the accident because he kept the first section of the freight in the snowshed for over thirty minutes without sending a flagman back down the track.[5] Despite such accidents, work continued at a fever pitch and such misfortunes were considered part of the sacrifice of empire building.

By September of 1882, the Denver, South Park, and Pacific finally succeeded in conquering Alpine Tunnel and arrived in Gunnison. The rails arrived just in time to give the Rio Grande some competition for a special excursion run which was being taken to the Denver Exposition.

Both railroads ran ads trying to entice tourists to observe the wonders of Alpine Tunnel and Marshall Pass. On September 3, in honor of "Gunnison Day" at the exposition, the Rio Grande ran a special of seven coach loads east over Marshall Pass, while the South Park took six coach loads through Alpine Tunnel. In all, between 500 and 800 residents of Gunnison went to Denver for the exposition. Two days later, Gunnison gave the South Park the welcoming celebration it had given the Rio Grande a year earlier. One pompous speaker, enjoying the exuberance of the moment, proclaimed that one railroad was a good thing, but that two railroads was even better because they would hold each other in check and force a lowering of freight rates. Actually, the South Park and the Rio Grande had already agreed that they had no desire to wage rate wars such as were going on within Jay Gould's Union Pacific system. Both roads had heavy construction debts and they had no intention of forcing rates below a profit making level.[6]

This is not to say that competition was not heavy between the South Park and Rio Grande. In July of 1884, a half-mile of snowsheds on the summit of Marshall Pass burned down. While there was no sufficient evidence for legal action, "it was immediately surmised that it was the work of incendiaries and the burning was, of course, coupled with the competition between the two roads." The track under the sheds was badly warped by the intense heat and the damage reached into the thousands of dollars. It was a week before any train could get over the pass; in the meantime, it was noted by suspicious individuals that the South Park got considerably more traffic through Alpine Tunnel. While the fire may have been started by sparks from a passing locomotive, the possibility of South Park arson provided more excitement and intrigue.[7]

Throughout this early period, the Denver and Rio Grande was constantly busy making improvements over Marshall Pass. Originally the rails over the pass were thirty pound steel—thirty pounds to the yard. In August of 1883, nine miles of the thirty pound steel were replaced by forty-five pound rails. Improvements were made in a cut three miles west of the summit and Chief Engineer McMurtrie made plans to replace many of the trestles and bridges which had been hurriedly built in 1881. With the replacement of the rails, the degree of curvature was reduced from twenty-four to fifteen degrees, lessening some of the hairpin windings and twistings of the road.[8]

Most of the laborers that made the improvements and worked on the Rio Grande's western extensions were first generation immigrants. A light-hearted scene occurred in July of 1889 on the summit of Marshall Pass when a free-for-all developed between a car load of Italian laborers and a car load of Celt laborers bound for work on the Rio Grande's western line. The lights were put out in the cars and many of the combatants received severe bruises. Just as the Italians started using knives, the ruckus was halted by "Doc" Shores, the famed Gunnison sheriff of the 1880s and later a detective for the Rio Grande. Shores restored order before anyone was seriously injured and sent the workers back to their respective cars.[9]

The initial boom of 1880 and 1881, when the Rio Grande system was able to charge almost any rate for a passage to the mines, declined as the whole country fell victim to a recession in 1883. Average passenger rates on the Rio Grande were as high as 7.27 cents per mile in 1880, but fell to 3.6 cents by 1883. The freight rates averaged 3.62 cents per ton per mile in 1881, but fell to 2.77 cents in 1884.[10] These rates were the average of the entire system and rates in mountainous terrain, such as Marshall Pass, were higher.

The fashionable and powerful travelled the rails with passes issued to them either because of their prestigious social position or because of important service rendered to the railroad. Some passes were issued for a year, while others were good for the holder's life time. Perhaps the most famous railroad passes were issued by Otto Mears for his Rio Grande Southern and Silverton lines. Rather than issue ordinary paper passes, Mears issued passes of finely engraved silver or elaborate leather. While the Rio Grande did not go to the extremes of Mears, it did issue its share of passes. In those days, catering to the important and those aspiring to importance was

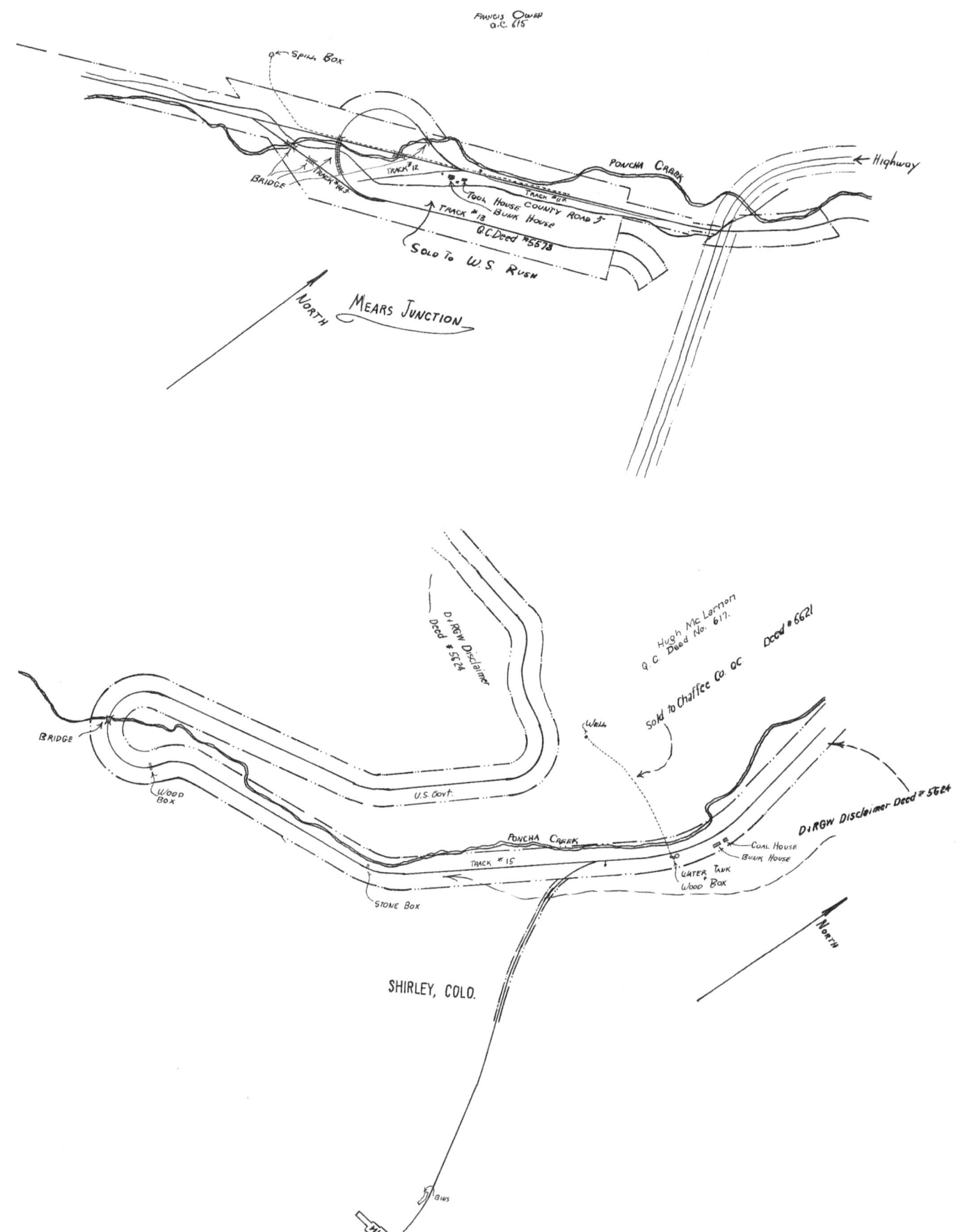

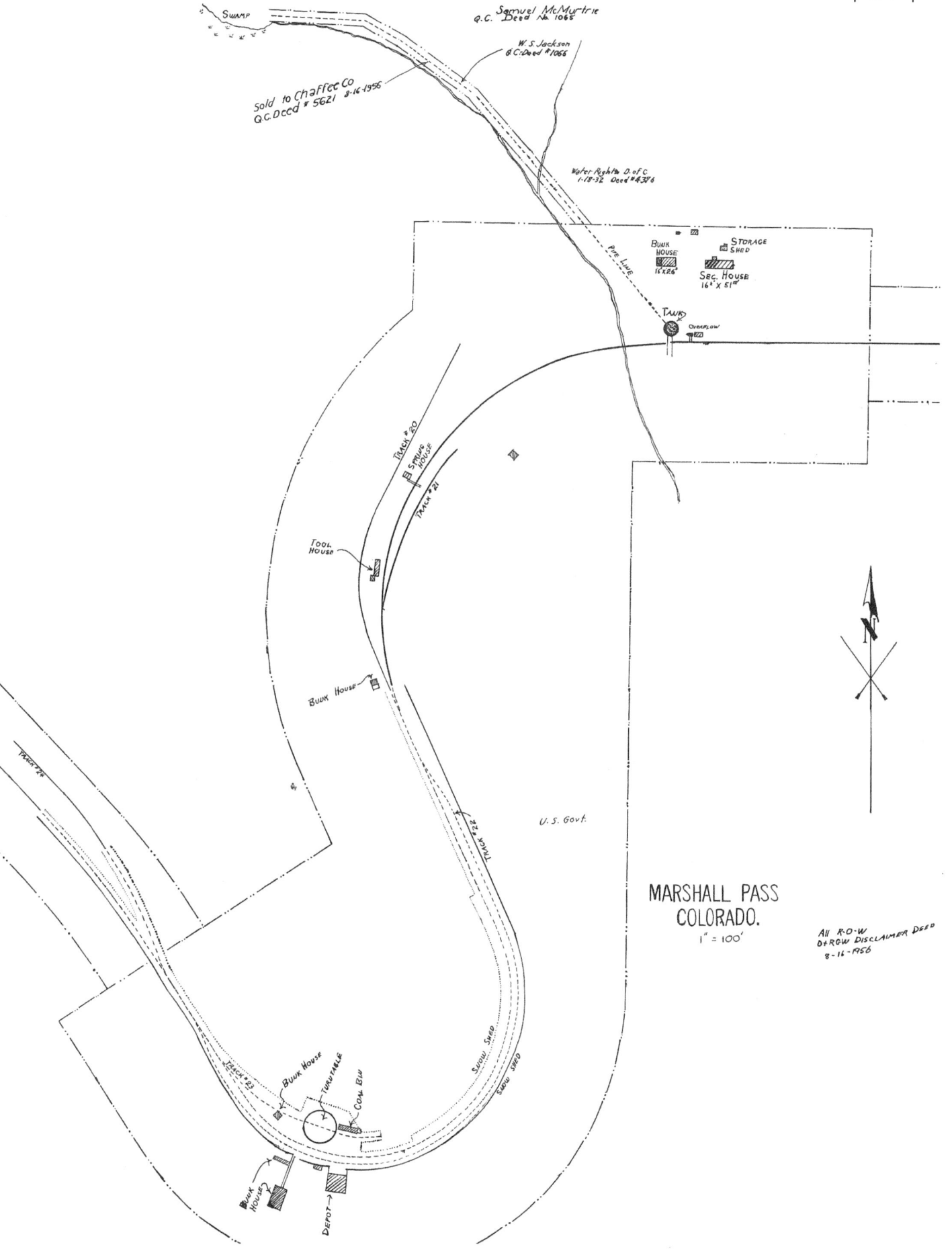

*Mears Junction, located exactly eleven miles from Salida, was the division point for traffic southbound via Poncha Pass for the San Luis Valley and westbound, via Marshall Pass, for the Gunnison country. The present highway crossing Poncha Pass curves through the center of the photo, passing directly in front of the square building at left.*
RICHARD A. RONZIO, DOW HELMERS COLLECTION

an integral part of railroad politics, and many obtained a pass for free transportation on the railroad. Thus, William Marshall entered the story once more.

While Marshall never made any claim to having located the exact route of the Rio Grande over Marshall Pass, his surveys were used considerably in the construction of the railroad over the pass. He felt that his having found the mountain pass entitled him to a railroad pass when he took his bride west on their honeymoon in 1884. Marshall wrote the general manager of the Rio Grande giving a brief resume of his exploits and requesting a pass to take him over the same country he had covered on foot eleven years earlier. The railroad replied with icy language that they could not issue a pass to anyone and everyone who claimed to have travelled a portion of their right-of-way, particularly when the person was foolish enough to have been in the mountains at that time of winter. Completely rebuffed, Marshall decided in a fit of rage to ignore the letter. Marshall told of the sequel to the incident in an interview with Thomas Dawson:

> *I scarcely thought of the incident again for almost another ten years, not, indeed, until 1893. In that year I had charge of the Engineer exhibit for the Government at the Chicago World's Fair. One morning while the Fair was in progress and while I was in Chicago, my attention was directed to a newspaper report of a speech which had been made by the Rio Grande manager at a Railroad congress the night before, in which he dwelt upon the embarrassments that subordinates sometimes cause to railroad managers. Judge my surprise when I found my own name mentioned and discovered that much prominence was given to the refusal of my pass application as an illustration of his point. He told of how the request had been received in his absence; how it had been dealt with by a smart young fellow new to the railroad business, who was temporarily in charge of the office routine; and then, capping the climax, how the youngster had gloated over the snub in reporting the facts to him.*[11]

The speaker went on to relate that Marshall's service to the Rio Grande had been so great that he would have gladly given him a lifetime pass. The manager's first impulse had been to write Marshall an explanation, but he decided to wait until Marshall replied. As time went by, the manager concluded that somehow Marshall had failed to receive the junior executive's saucy letter, and, pleased to escape from the predicament, he let the matter drop. This was sufficient explanation for Marshall and he sought out the gentleman to have a hearty laugh. Things were quite different in 1910 when Marshall, then a general in the Corps of Engineers, rode over Marshall Pass in a special car as the guest of the Rio Grande.[12]

If Marshall had gotten the original pass he requested and ridden over Marshall Pass in 1884, he undoubtedly would have been amazed by the changes that had taken place since his visit of 1873. From Salida, the railroad ran west five miles to Poncha Springs. At Poncha Springs, the railroad curved south up the valley of Poncha Creek along present-day U. S. 285 four and one-half miles to the small station of Otto. Otto, named after Otto Mears, was one and one-half miles below Mears Junction where the Marshall Pass line turned west to cross Marshall Pass and the Rio Grande line climbed south over Poncha Pass into the San Luis Valley. Some historians claim that Mears Junction was named not for the "Pathfinder of the San Juans," but for Dave Mears who had been with Marshall on the pass in 1873. Whatever the railroad's intentions in naming the junction, time has forgotten Dave Mears. The junction at Mears was a key point in railroad operations for helper engines on both Marshall and Poncha Passes, as well as a switching point for the two lines.

Two and one-half miles above Mears, Shirley had passed through the boom of 1881 and settled into the role of a siding and tank town. In railroad slang, tank town referred derogatorily to a place whose only existence stemmed from the importance of its water tank. In the era of steam locomotives, water was a critical necessity and Marshall Pass was dotted with tank towns. Keene, three and one-half miles west of Shirley, was not even a tank town; its sole importance came from its nineteen-car capacity siding. Keene was 600 vertical feet higher than Shirley. The railroad made a long loop to the south and then a series of smaller loops to the north in the process of gaining elevation. From Keene, the road hugged the mountainside and wound around the site of present-day O'Haver Lake to Grays Siding or simply Grays. Grays was six miles from

*Nestled beneath the great cirque of Mount Ouray, Grays Siding was a key water tank and siding between Mears Junction and the summit of Marshall Pass.*

C. H. CLARK PHOTO, DOW HELMERS COLLECTION

*Barely visible across the distant skyline are the peaks of the Sangre de Cristo range, seen from the highest point of Marshall Pass. The railroad crossed the pass just out of the picture at bottom right. Taking water at the tank is one of the tiny 100 series engines.*
WILLIAM H. JACKSON PHOTO, CHARLES LEAMING TUTT LIBRARY; DOW HELMERS COLLECTION

*A road engine and helper pulling two baggage cars and three coaches emerge from a snowshed covering one of the cuts between Grays Siding and the summit.*
DENVER PUBLIC LIBRARY - WESTERN HISTORY DEPARTMENT

*Seventeen cars on the great loop above Shirley. Alongside Poncha Creek, below, is a portion of Otto Mears's Marshall Pass wagon road.*
ROBERT W. RICHARDSON PHOTO. DOW HELMERS COLLECTION

*Three engines move twenty-seven cars, upgrade just beyond Shirley, on the east side of Marshall Pass. One leg of the Shirley wye can be seen at lower right.*
WILLIAM H. JACKSON PHOTO; DENVER PUBLIC LIBRARY - WESTERN HISTORY DEPARTMENT;
DOW HELMERS COLLECTION

*After pulling away, upgrade, from the great loop at Shirley, the grade passed through a large cut, to emerge with this awesome view, looking back to Mears Junction, in the distance.*
DOW HELMERS COLLECTION

the summit of the pass and was an important half-way point. In addition to the water tower and fuel station, Grays's forty-six car siding provided a place for passenger trains half-way up the grade to pass slow moving freights and work trains. From Grays the road twisted up the shoulder of Mount Ouray as the valley of Poncha Creek dropped away below. The station of Pocono was located half-way between Grays and the summit. Its very location, wedged near the railroad below the slopes of Mount Ouray and above the depths of the valley, suggests that it was little more than a name on the Rio Grande's time table.

The summit of the pass was characterized by a unique three-quarter of a mile straightaway on the eastern slope. Nestled on the eastern slope against the hogback ridge of the summit was the water tower and two large buildings housing railroad personnel and the station. At these buildings the road curved south and crossed the Continental Divide through the cut that had been blasted out in 1881. During the 1880s, snowsheds covered the track through the cut and down the western slope for more than a mile. Just across the Divide as the track curved to the north, another cluster of buildings was located on the south of the road. These included a tall lookout tower, which could scan the entire sixteen miles of the western slope. To the north and running parallel to the mainline was another siding with a capacity of sixty-two cars.

On the western slope the roadbed twisted down no less than five major terraces in dropping the 1400 feet to Chester, half-way down the slope to Sargent. Half-way between the summit and Chester was Shawano. Named after a Ute Chief, the stop had the usual characteristics of a water tank and siding. The Shawano Loop was one of the scenic attractions on the pass as it not only gave the passengers the sensation of having turned around, paralleling the track they had just been over, but also offered a view of the winding road below. George A. Crofutt in *Crofutt's Overland Tours*, referring to a visit to Colorado and the West, paid particular attention to this engineering marvel.

> ... the rail tracks above and below seem to be running in all directions; and you are led to query what other railroad companies have built over this pass, when you suddenly discover that some of the tracks are those over which you have lately passed, and others are those over which you will presently pass.[13]

From Chester the track ran two miles to Tank Seven, so named because of its location seven miles above Sargent. By Tank Seven, the worst of the pass was over and the railroad had six and one-half miles of easy running to make the remaining distance to Sargent through the stations of Buxton and Jackson Spur.

Sargent was the key point on the west just as Mears Junction was on the east. Aside from the water tank and siding space for 155 cars, the town was the headquarters of the helper engines on the western slope and boasted a six-stall roundhouse. Named Marshalltown when founded in 1880, it survived a weak attempt by the Denver and Rio Grande to rename it Aureau, and finally adopted the name of the town's leading merchant, Joseph Sargents. His hotel and eating house were popular with Rio Grande crews and passengers until it was destroyed by a fire on New Year's Eve, 1882. From Mears Junction to Sargent, all of the stations and tank stops had one thing in common; their existence was tied explicitly to the railroad. At some of the stations, a few head of cattle grazed, such as in the rich pasture lands around Tank Seven, and at some of the lower stations, vegetable gardens were planted to supplement meals, but the economy of the towns on Marshall Pass could be summarized in one word— railroad!

What was it like to travel across Marshall Pass on the Denver and Rio Grande during the peak years of its glory? One of the most glamorous accounts of such a journey may be found in Ernest Ingersoll's *The Crest of the Continent*. Ingersoll spent the summer of 1883 traveling on the railroads of the Rocky Mountains and then published *The Crest of the Continent* in 1885 telling

## →THE SCENIC LINE OF AMERICA,←
# THE DENVER & RIO GRANDE RAILWAY,

With its numerous branches and extensions penetrating all sections of Colorado and northern New Mexico, forms the greatest system of Narrow Gauge Railway in the world, and affords Tourists, Invalids, and Business Travel

### THE BEST, AND IN MANY INSTANCES THE ONLY ROUTE

To the leading Health and Pleasure Resorts of the Rocky Mountains, and to the Richest Mining Regions and most Important Cities of the Mid-Continent.

### FOR BUSINESS:

**DENVER, COLORADO SPRINGS, PUEBLO,**

Cañon City, South Arkansas, Alpine, Buena Vista, Leadville, Kokomo, Red Cliff, Gunnison City, Silver Cliff, El Moro; Alamosa, Antonito, Durango, Silverton, Taos, Espanola, Santa Fe, and the marvelous San Juan and Gunnison Countries.

### FOR HEALTH AND PLEASURE:

Manitou, Garden of the Gods, Pike's Peak, Royal Gorge, Poncho Springs, Brown's Cañon, Cottonwood Springs, Twin Lakes, Veta Pass, Wagon Wheel Gap, Toltec Gorge, Phantom Curve, Los Pinos Valley, Pagosa Springs, Ojo Caliente, Comanche Cañon, Cave Dwellings, Aztec Ruins, &c.

### →THE MOUNTAIN SCENERY←

Of this Line is unequaled in variety and grandeur by that of any other railway on either hemisphere, and the hotels at the attractive points are the best west of the Missouri River.

Two daily Express Trains, equipped with Pullman Palace Sleepers, Horton Reclining Chair Cars, Elegant Regular Coaches, Model Open Observation Cars, Westinghouse Air-Brakes, and running over Steel Rails, Iron Bridges and Rock Ballast, insure the highest type of rapid, safe, and luxurious railway travel.

The Denver & Rio Grande Railway, with its eastern connections at Pueblo and Denver, forms the shortest route by many miles, and the quickest by over ten hours' time, between all points East, and the interior of Colorado.

NEARLY 800 MILES IN OPERATION, AND THE ONLY LINE UNDER COLORADO MANAGEMENT

D. C. DODGE,
*General Manager.*

F. C. NIMS,
*General Passenger and Ticket Agent.*

DENVER, COLO.

*"The only line under Colorado management" the Denver & Rio Grande Railway, published this persuasive advertisement widely, circa 1885, including publication in George Crofutt's* Grip Sack Guide of Colorado.

Dow Helmers Collection

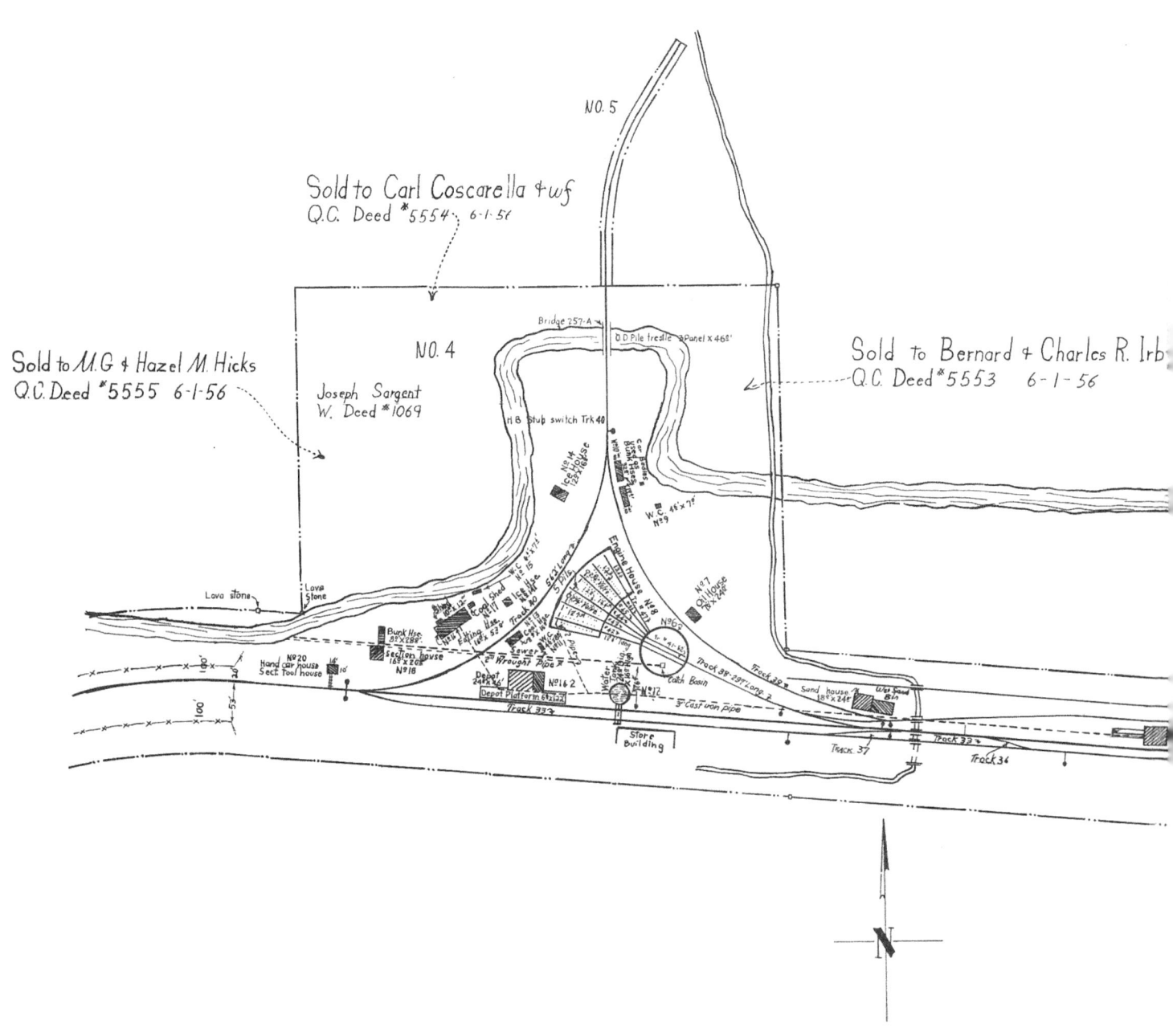

*Engine 489 taking coal at the coaling platform at Sargent.*
ROBERT W. RICHARDSON PHOTO, DOW HELMERS COLLECTION

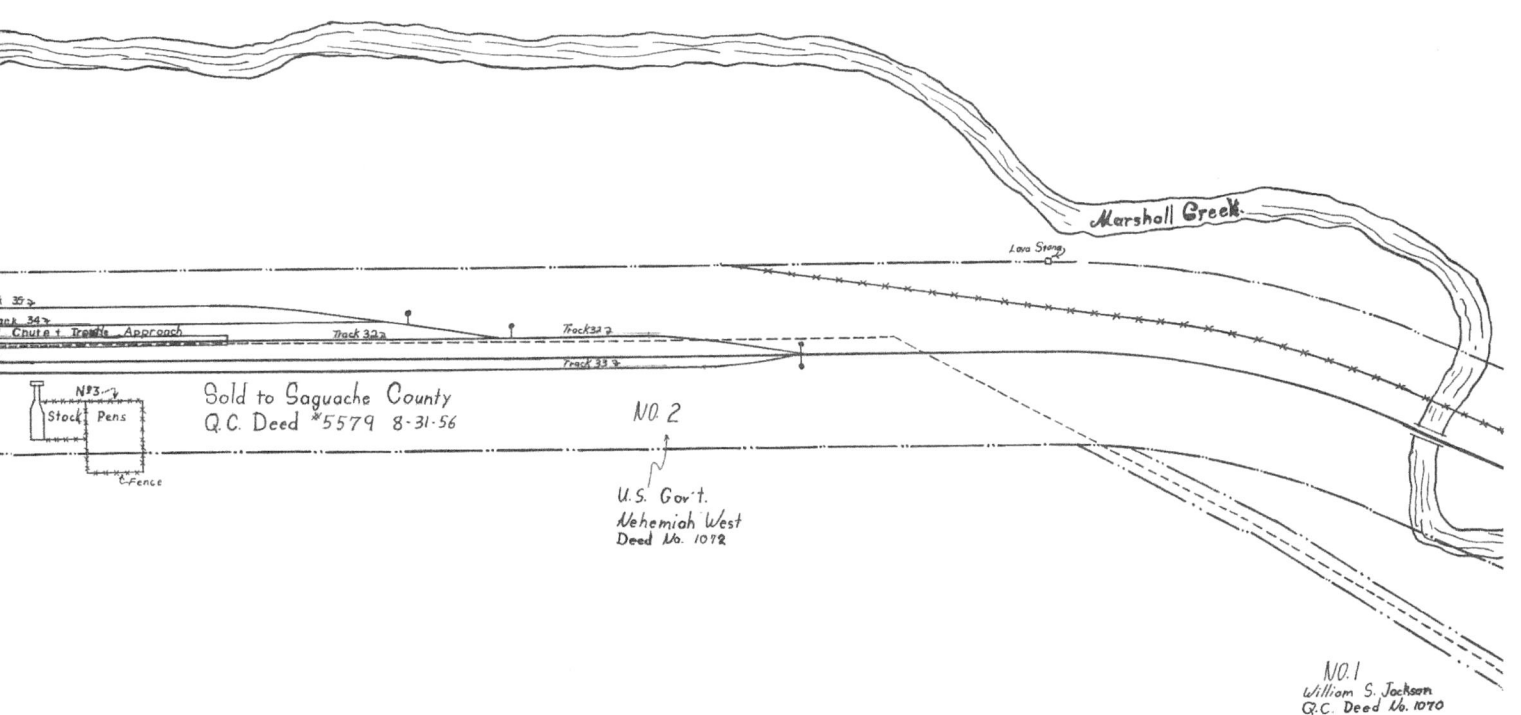

# Denver & Rio Grande Railroad.

## TRAINS BETWEEN DENVER AND GRAND JUNCTION.

| WEST | | | | | EAST | | |
|---|---|---|---|---|---|---|---|
| °No. 25 Way Freig't SE. | °No. 23 Way Freig't SE. | No. 7 Pacific Express D | Miles. | STATIONS. | No. 8 Atlantic Express D | °No. 22 Way Freig't D | °No. 24 Way Freig't SE. |
| ......... | * | 8 20 | ......... | Le......Denver......Ar | 9 10 | * | ......... |
| ......... | * | 1 10 | 119.6 | ......Pueblo...... | 4 13 | * | ......... |
| ......... | 6 40 | †ar5 00 | 216.5 | N......Salida...... | ‡lv 12 25 | 4 55 | lv5 05 |
| ......... | ......... | †lv5 10 | ......... | ...... | ‡ar 12 05 | ......... | ar5 00 |
| ......... | 7 05 | * 5 23 | 221.5 | D......Poncha Jc...... | * 11 53 | 4 30 | 4 38 |
| ......... | 7 30 | 5 39 | 226.0 | ......Otto...... | 11 36 | 3 56 | 4 09 |
| ......... | 7 45 | * 5 46 | 227.5 | D......Mears Jc...... | * 11 30 | 3 45 | 4 00 |
| ......... | 7 58 | † 5 55 | 229.7 | ......Shirley...... | † 11 20 | 3 25 | 3 42 |
| ......... | 8 22 | 6 12 | 233.4 | ......Keene...... | 11 03 | 3 02 | 3 20 |
| ......... | 8 34 | † 6 20 | 235.5 | D......Gray's...... | † 10 55 | 2 48 | 3 08 |
| ......... | 8 55 | 6 35 | 239.0 | ......Pocono...... | 10 40 | 2 23 | 2 45 |
| ......... | 9 15 | ar6 48 | 242.2 | N....Marshall Pass.... | lv 10 25 | lv 2 00 | lv 2 25 |
| ......... | 9 30 | lv6 55 | ......... | ...... | ar 10 15 | ar 1 50 | ar2 15 |
| ......... | 9 57 | 7 08 | 245.3 | ......Hillden...... | 9 57 | 1 20 | 1 50 |
| ......... | 10 05 | 7 13 | 246.4 | D......Shawano...... | 9 50 | 1 10 | 1 40 |
| ......... | 10 30 | † 7 28 | 250.1 | D......Chester...... | † 9 30 | 12 35 | 1 17 |
| ......... | 11 05 | 7 47 | 254.3 | ......Buxton...... | 9 15 | 11 59 | 12 50 |
| ......... | 11 35 | †ar8 00 | 258.9 | N......Sargent...... | † lv 9 00 | lv 11 30 | lv 12 20 |
| ......... | 12 01 | †lv8 20 | ......... | ...... | ‡ ar 8 55 | ar 11 05 | ar 11 55 |
| ......... | 12 28 | 8 29 | 263.5 | ......Elko...... | 8 45 | 10 44 | 11 28 |
| ......... | 12 50 | † 8 37 | 267.2 | ......Crookton...... | † 8 37 | 10 28 | 11 08 |
| ......... | 1 08 | † 8 46 | 271.0 | ......Doyle...... | † 8 28 | 10 11 | 10 46 |
| ......... | 1 13 | 8 48 | 272.1 | ......Bonita...... | 8 26 | 10 07 | 10 40 |
| ......... | 1 45 | † 9 01 | 278.5 | D......Parlin...... | † 8 12 | 9 40 | 10 05 |
| ......... | 2 10 | 9 12 | 283.8 | ......Mounds...... | 7 58 | 9 12 | 9 35 |
| ......... | 2 40 | ar9 25 | 290.3 | N......Gunnison...... | lv 7 45 | lv8 40 | 9 00 |
| 7 50 | ......... | lv9 30 | ......... | ...... | ar 7 25 | ar8 10 | ......... |
| ......... | ......... | 9 44 | 296.1 | ......Ridgway...... | 7 08 | 7 45 | ......... |
| 8 15 | ......... | 9 57 | 301.7 | D......Kezar...... | † 6 53 | 7 18 | ......... |
| 8 40 | ......... | † 10 14 | 308.8 | ......Cebolla...... | 6 33 | 6 42 | ......... |
| 9 10 | ......... | * 10 35 | 315.8 | D......Sapinero...... | * 6 13 | 6 10 | ......... |
| 9 45 | ......... | † 10 57 | 322.5 | D......Curecanti...... | † 6 51 | 5 37 | ......... |
| 10 20 | ......... | 11 18 | 329.2 | ......Crystal Creek...... | 5 30 | 5 07 | ......... |
| 10 56 | ......... | ar11 23 | 330.8 | N......Cimarron...... | lv 5 25 | lv5 00 | ......... |
| ar 11 05 | ......... | lv11 28 | ......... | ...... | ar 5 20 | ar4 30 | ......... |
| lv 11 20 | ......... | * 11 55 | 336.4 | D....Cerro Summit.... | * 4 55 | 3 55 | ......... |
| 12 10 | ......... | † 12 20 | 342.9 | D......Cedar Creek...... | † 4 23 | 3 10 | ......... |
| 12 50 | ......... | 12 33 | 347.0 | ......Fairview...... | 4 05 | 2 30 | ......... |
| 1 22 | ......... | ar 12 46 | 353.2 | N......Montrose...... | lv 3 50 | lv2 00 | ......... |
| ar 1 50 | ......... | lv 12 50 | ......... | ...... | ar 3 45 | ar1 50 | ......... |
| lv 2 00 | ......... | 1 02 | 359.0 | ......Menoken...... | 3 29 | 1 23 | ......... |
| 2 25 | ......... | † 1 13 | 364.0 | ......Colorow...... | † 3 16 | 1 00 | ......... |
| 2 48 | ......... | 1 23 | 369.0 | ......Chipeta...... | 3 02 | 12 36 | ......... |
| 3 11 | ......... | * 1 38 | 374.5 | N......Delta...... | * 2 47 | 12 10 | ......... |
| 3 40 | ......... | † 1 50 | 379.2 | D......Roubideau...... | † 2 32 | 11 30 | ......... |
| 4 01 | ......... | 1 57 | 381.7 | ......Duncan...... | 2 26 | 11 19 | ......... |
| 4 13 | ......... | 2 12 | 386.5 | ......Escalente...... | 2 12 | 10 58 | ......... |
| 4 36 | ......... | * 2 27 | 392.3 | ......Dominguez...... | * 1 58 | 10 28 | ......... |
| 5 07 | ......... | 2 43 | 399.2 | N......Bridgeport...... | * 1 42 | 9 58 | ......... |
| 5 43 | ......... | 2 54 | 404.1 | ......Deer Run...... | 1 30 | 9 36 | ......... |
| 6 06 | ......... | † 3 07 | 409.1 | ......Kahnah...... | † 1 17 | 9 12 | ......... |
| 6 31 | ......... | † 3 16 | 412.8 | D......Whitewater...... | † 1 08 | 8 56 | ......... |
| 6 50 | ......... | 3 28 | 418.3 | ......Unaweep...... | 12 56 | 8 30 | ......... |
| 7 17 | ......... | ar 3 45 | 425.2 | Ar. N....Grand J....Le | lv 12 40 | lv 8 00 | ......... |
| 7 50 | ......... | lv 3 55 | ......... | ...... | ar 12 30 | ar | ......... |

For explanation of terms, see page 5.
Mountain Time (105th Mer.) the Standard, furnished by A. B. Ingols, Jeweler, 1614 Larimer St., Denver.

*November 1887 Public Timetable.*

about his experiences. In his book Ingersoll gave particular detail to the nature of the land and the engineering difficulties of the route.

> One of the wonders of Colorado Progress is the Gunnison valley. The "Gunnison" as it is usually termed, embraces a wide area, being in popular parlance, everything in Colorado west of the Continental Divide, north of the San Juan mountains and south of the Eagle river district.
>
> It is by way of Marshall Pass that the railway enters the Gunnison. Leaving the main line and the Arkansas valley at Salida, only five miles are traversed before the train begins to enter Poncha Pass and climb the mountains, which it requires four hours, express speed, to cross,—four hours of uninterrupted pleasure.
>
> Marshall Pass itself, which we enter imperceptibly out of Poncha, is a depression in the main range and lies between Ouray and Exchequer mountains. It was a daring scheme to run the road over here—for through wouldn't press it properly. The summit is almost eleven thousand feet above the sea, and timber line is so close that you can think sometimes you are actually there. The trees are stunted and all stand bent at an angle, showing the direction of the fierce and prevalant [sic] winds that have pressed upon them from their seedling days. The cones they bear start bravely, but after perfecting three or four broad circles of scales and seeds the nipping frosts of August and September admonish them to make haste; so the remainder of the cone is put forth so hastily, in nature's attempt to complete her work, that the whole remaining length of fifteen or twenty circlets will not exceed the length of the first two or three full grown scales, and the cone ends ridiculously in a little useless acuminate tip.
>
> To attain this height, the road has to twist and wriggle in the most confusing way, going three or four miles, sometimes, to make fifty rods (825 feet); but all the time it gains ground upward, over some startling bridges, along the crest of huge fillings, through miniature canons blasted out of rock or shoveled through gravel, and always up slopes whose steepness it needs no practiced eye to appreciate. To say that the road crosses a pass in the Rocky Mountains 10,820 feet in height is enough to astonish the conservative engineers who have never seen this audacious line; but you can magnify their amazement when you tell them that some of the grades are 220 feet to the mile.
>
> The mountains and hills in the neighborhood of Marshall Pass are clothed for the most part with grass, or else sagebrush and weeds, and with timber, scant in some places, dense in others. The tourist will not see there the startling cliffs and chasms that break up the mountains on the road to Durango, but, on the other hand, he will not feel any terror at dizzy precipices, nor tremble lest some toppling pinnacle should fall upon his fragile car. No better exhibition of the greatness and breadth of these mountains could be found, however, than here. There are stretches away beneath and around you and endless series of hills, some rounded and entirely overgrown with dark woods, others rising into a comb-like crest, or rearing a dome-shaped head above the possibilities of timber-growth and covered with a smooth cap of yellowing verdure. They crowd one another on every side, and brace themselves, each by each, as though their broad and solid foundations were not enough for safety. They stand cheek by jowl in sturdy companionship, taking rain and sunny weather, hurtling storms and serene days with impartial equality. Your vision will not find the limit of these huge hills until it is cut off by the serrated horizon of the crest of the Sangre de Cristo, or by some frowning monarch near at hand, holding his head high and venerably gray, as becomes a chieftain, where he can get the first messages of the gods and be looked up to by a thousand of his more humble kin.

"It is like a huge green sea," murmurs the Madame, hitherto silent with gazing. "I know a great many people have made the same comparison before—have often said that these commingled ranges were as a sea, tossing its white crests here and there all at once congealed; but that is the very impression which fixes itself upon you. These rounded, or sharp-edged, tumultuous mountains are like a wide, green ocean." The great cone on the northern side of the track close to which the roadway skirts nearly the whole distance through the pass, is Ouray Peak. Ouray was the head chief of the Utes. This tribe only lately abandoned all this portion of Colorado. The peak we have hugged so closely does honor to the dead chief. The farther you get around it the more nobly do its proportions rise into the blue ether. This peak is of white volcanic rock that has decomposed into small blocks. The sides then are loose "slides," as steep as the fragmentary stuff will lie, and the top is a narrow summit with smooth, rounded outlines. We are only a few hundred feet from the topmost timber, yet the bald white summit rears its head to almost unmeasured heights above, and claims our admiration by its simple majesty, far more than does the broken, cliff furnished upthrust or Exchequer Peak, opposite, though its black head is held quite as high.

On our way to the summit we had crawled through long snowsheds, built to protect the road from the snows of winter, and which are hung late in spring with brilliant icicles formed by the sun without and the cold within. Passing through the last shed, which has a length of fully half a mile, we reached the highest point of the divide and while the extra engine which had helped pull us up the steep grades went cautiously down the valley toward Gunnison before us, we climbed the rocks about the little station house, to enjoy at its best the magnificent view presented.

Far below we could look down on four lines of our road, terrace below terrace, the last so far down the mountain as to be quite indistinct to the view. The iron loops were lost to sight at times as the road wound about some interfering hill; and often the forest was so dense that the track seemed to have disappeared forever. Five hundred feet down the mountainside we could see a water tank, and knew that it marked the spot where we would be, after an hour of twisting down the incline. As we gazed upon the mountains, the valley, and the farther heights, we could imagine ourselves returned to the beginning of things, and shown the globe only that moment finished. There was a wealth of coloring, a sublimity unsurpassed, and withal an attention given to detail by which the picture was made perfect.[14]

This dramatic painting of a run over Marshall Pass was commissioned to famed railroad artist Otto Kuhler by Dr. Robert C. Black III, a noted Colorado historian, who sought to remember an excursion he had taken over the pass as a young boy.
DOW HELMERS COLLECTION

*Looking north along the crest of the Continental Divide, the summit snowsheds and buildings are visible. Note the series of snowsheds extending far down the western slope.*
WILLIAM H. JACKSON PHOTO, COLORADO HISTORICAL SOCIETY; DOW HELMERS COLLECTION

Standing on the summit of Marshall Pass with the sun setting behind a curtain of flame to the west, Ingersoll was awed by the brilliant reflections and long shadows of the mountains as nature prepared to sleep. The peace of mind and tranquility which he felt prompted him to remark that "all outward things and inward thoughts teemed with assurances of immortality." Indeed, the extremes of Marshall Pass were brought into sharp focus by comparing the warmth and beauty of Ingersoll's account with the reminiscences of the men who bucked the freights through the blinding snow and freezing cold of a Colorado winter.

> *Our descent from the pass was continuous but slow. At least it was slow at first. All steam was shut off in the engine and the air-brakes were used to preserve uniform speed. Winding in and out among the trees, and catching at different times extended views of the Tomichi, we worked our way to more level country and were soon skirting the meadows and whirling across the ranch properties of the fertile valley.*[15]

A few years after Ingersoll's journey, no less a celebrity than Rudyard Kipling journeyed across Marshall Pass and found the ride equally thrilling.

> *Next day ... myself and a few others began the real ascent of the Rockies; up to that time our climbing didn't count. The train ran violently up a steep place and was taken to pieces. Five cars were hitched onto two locomotives, and two cars to one locomotive. This seemed to be a kind and thoughtful act, but I was idiot enough to go forward and watch the coupling-on of the two cars in which Caesar and his fortunes were to travel. Some one had lost or eaten the regularly ordained coupling, and a man picked up from the tailboard of the engine a single iron link about as thick as a fetter-link watch-chain, and "guessed it would do." Get hauled up a Simla cliff by the hook of a lady's parasol if you wish to appreciate my sentiments when the cars moved uphill and the link drew tight. Miles away and two thousand feet above our heads rose the shoulder of a*

*hill epauletted with the long line of a snow tunnel. The first section of the cars crawled a quarter of a mile ahead of us, the track snaked and looped behind, and there was a black drop to the left. So we went up and up and up till the thin air grew thinner and the* chunk -chunk-chunk, *of the labouring locomotive was answered by the oppressed beating of the exhausted heart. Through the chequed light and shade of the snow tunnels (horrible caverns of rude timbering) we ground our way, halting now and again to allow a down train to pass. One monster of forty mineral-cars slid past, scarce held by four locomotives, their brakes screaming and chortling in chorus; and in the end, after a glimpse of half America spread map-wise leagues below us, we halted at the head of the longest snow tunnel of all, on the crest of the divide, between ten and eleven thousand feet above the level of the sea.*

*The locomotive wished to draw breath, and passengers to gather the flowers that nodded impertinently through the chinks of the boarding. A lady passenger's nose began to bleed, and the other ladies threw themselves down on the seats and gasped with the gasping train, while a wind as keen as a knife-edge rioted down the grimy tunnel.*

*Then dispatching a pilot-engine to clear the way, we began the downward portion of the journey with every available brake on, and frequent shrieks, till after some hours we reached the level plain.*[16]

Rare indeed was the passenger who travelled Marshall Pass in good weather and failed to appreciate the magnificent beauty and engineering accomplishments of the route. The scenery of Marshall Pass and the Royal Gorge to the east and the Black Canyon of the Gunnison to the west prompted the Rio Grande to adopt the slogan, "Scenic Line of America." In 1884, Shadrach K. Hooper, General Passenger and Ticket Agent of the Rio Grande, went one step

*The scenic wonders of Marshall Pass were always a drawing card for tourists. This crowd posed for William Henry Jackson's camera on August 25, 1885.*

WILLIAM H. JACKSON PHOTO. COLORADO HISTORICAL SOCIETY

*An engine pulling the first section of a passenger train puffs out of one of the snowsheds on the "Shawano Loop." It is easy to see that the passengers were justified in their complaints that the coaches filled with smoke during the passage through a shed. The snowsheds on the final mile to the summit are visible in the background.*

COLORADO HISTORICAL SOCIETY

further and changed the slogan to read the "Scenic Line of the World," adopting as its symbol the Curecanti Needle of the Black Canyon. Praise was lavished upon this route from all quarters. In speaking of the Rio Grande system, *Harper's Weekly* boasted that "Marshall Pass is perhaps better known than any other point by reason of its great height, its magnificent scenery, and the difficulty with which it is climbed, to say nothing of the fact that it is on the through line of the road between Denver and Ogden."[17] Marshall Pass also received publicity in the *New York Times* when the paper proclaimed in 1893 that the pass was the most famous of the Denver and Rio Grande's climbs.[18]

As the Rio Grande profited from the tourist trade and freight traffic over Marshall Pass, an event occurred in 1890 which foretold the eventual end of the Marshall Pass line. Growing traffic on the Rio Grande had persuaded Palmer to convert the line from Denver to Pueblo to standard gauge in 1881. In 1890, the railroad laid a third rail from Pueblo to Leadville, permitting either standard gauge or narrow gauge equipment to operate on it. Better equipment, improved construction techniques, and rival competitors dictated that in the future the building and improvements along the main lines be standard gauge. So it was that in 1890 the Rio Grande completed a standard gauge line from Leadville over Tennessee Pass and on down the valley of the Colorado River through Glenwood Springs and Rifle to Grand Junction. While it was some time before this new standard gauge line adversely affected the Marshall Pass branch, the trend toward standard gauge was set. Just as important was the fact that now the Rio Grande had two lines across the Continental Divide. Marshall Pass retained a substantial volume of tourist traffic and did a big business in local freight, but the majority of through traffic between

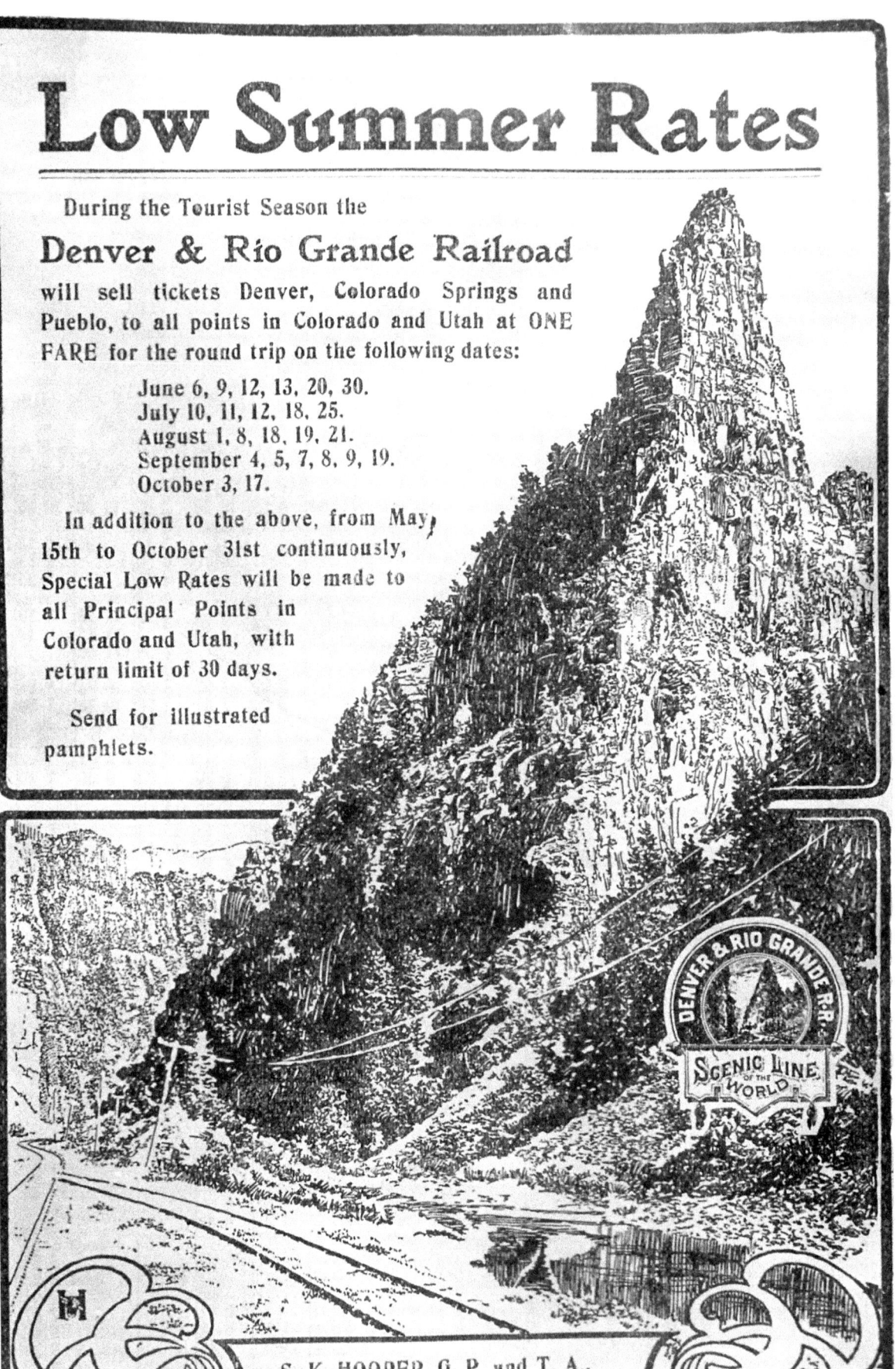

Advertisement "Rocky Mountain Official Railway Guide" December, 1904.
DOW HELMERS COLLECTION

Denver and Salt Lake City went by way of Tennessee Pass, where it could be carried on standard gauge rails all the way.

In late July of 1890, as if in protest of the new route over Tennessee Pass, a disastrous fire hit the summit of Marshall Pass. Probably caused by a flying cinder, the fire destroyed the station, telegraph office, agent's residence and some snowsheds. After the fire had burned itself out, the ruins were quickly cleared away and the tracks repaired.[18] In an era of cut-throat competition, the Rio Grande could ill afford to have its main line through central Colorado blocked. If the economy of the Marshall Pass line needed a shot in the arm after 1890, it got it from the Denver, South Park, and Pacific. After the South Park's arrival in Gunnison in September of 1882, the road had competed with the Rio Grande for Gunnison traffic using its route through the Alpine Tunnel. Poor management of the South Park in the late 1880s caused a neglect of the route. Consequently, when a rockslide in Alpine Tunnel caused the route to be closed from 1888 to 1895, the Rio Grande carried South Park traffic from Nathrop to Gunnison by way of Marshall Pass.

As the entire country underwent a financial crisis in 1893, the Rio Grande, reorganized in 1886 as the Denver and Rio Grande *Railroad*, mirrored the economic position of the nation. Yet, thanks to the popular tourist trade and the great volume of local freight, the Marshall Pass line did not suffer greatly. A timetable for July 30, 1893, showed the line busy with three main trains heading each direction each day. Heading eastward from Gunnison schedules ran as follows: the Colorado Express, a first-class passenger train, left Gunnison at 4:00 P. M. daily and

*Salida, Colorado from Tenderfoot Hill looking up F Street. At left D&RG depot; at right, steel trestle takes rails on narrow gauge to Marshall Pass and the tracks to right to Malta and Tennessee Pass. Train in foreground has stopped for lunch at the Monte Christo Hotel.*

WILLIAM HENRY JACKSON PHOTO, DOW HELMERS COLLECTION

*In 1890, two years before the great fire, the Salida round house and shop throbbed with activity twenty-four hours a day. On the "go out" track are 207, 429 and 711. Twenty engines are counted, making Salida one of the busiest rail terminals in all of Colorado.*    COURTESY MRS. W. R. THOMPSON. DOW HELMERS COLLECTION

arrived in Salida just four hours later at 8:00 P. M.; the Colorado Fast-Freight, a freight with connections on east to Denver, left Gunnison at 4:30 P. M. daily and with stops for loading and unloading, arrived in Salida at 11:20 P. M.; the local freight, serving local commerce along the line, left Gunnison at 8:25 A. M. and after a day's journey of slowly winding over Marshall Pass picking up and distributing freight along the way, arrived in Salida at 4:00 P. M.[20] Of course, numerous difficulties made this schedule impossible to follow, particularly during the winter, and at times mass confusion resulted when the schedules of westbound trains were integrated with the above schedule. It was then that the ten sidings between Mears Junction and Sargent became important.

If Marshall Pass was not drastically affected by the Panic of 1893, other problems, such as the labor disputes which rocked the country in the 1880s and 1890s, came to Marshall Pass. An incident during the summer of 1894 produced an interesting experience for D. J. McCanne, a Gunnison businessman. McCanne had been in Denver on business and was planning to return to Gunnison in time for the Fourth of July celebrations when a strike of railroad firemen virtually crippled the entire Rio Grande system. By getting some firemen to serve incognito to fire the engines the railroad was able to make its run to Salida from Denver, although much behind schedule. Not wishing to spend July 4 in Salida, McCanne, a mine foreman, and a Rio Grande engineer set off to walk across Marshall Pass.

# The Way to Reach Gunnison County Colorado

is by way of

# DENVER & RIO GRANDE

"Scenic Line of the World."

Curecanti Needle
Black Canon of the Gunnison

AFTER leaving Denver the traveler from the East en route to Gunnison County passes through Colorado Springs, Pueblo, Canon City and the famous Royal Gorge. At Salida change of train is made and the eastern slope of Marshall Pass, the crossing of the Continental Divide is scaled; and then down the western slope the train traverses Gunnison County, rich in industrial resources and scenic attractions. The route parallels the Gunnison River, the most noted trout stream in America, and penetrates the wonderful Black Canon of the Gunnison.

The traveler from Salt Lake City, Ogden or the West makes connection for the Gunnison-Marshall Pass Line at Grand Junction.

Information regarding train schedules, fares and the resources and scenic attractions of the Rocky Mountain region will be gladly furnished by any Rio Grande Passenger Representative, or,

**Frank A. Wadleigh, Passenger Traffic Manager**
Denver, Colorado

*Circa, 1916.*

#406 pauses near the main summit snowshed (right) on the eastern summit siding.
ROBERT M. DAVIS PHOTO, COLORADO HISTORICAL SOCIETY

This view looks west past the summit snowsheds and siding to Shawano. The Shawano water tank is visible in the center of the picture as are two sets of snowsheds on the "Shawano Loop."
DENVER PUBLIC LIBRARY - WESTERN HISTORY DEPARTMENT

After spending the evening of July 3 at Mears Junction, the party with several additions set off on the morning of the Fourth for the summit. While most of the group followed the railroad grade, McCanne and a companion followed the gullies and Grays Creek up to Grays Siding. There they rejoined the rest of the group and walked the remaining six miles to the summit. At the top they got unexpected help from Rio Grande Superintendent Arthur Ridgway, who telegraphed orders for the group to be taken down the west side of the pass by handcar, a ride which McCanne later spoke of with great excitement. Once west of Sargent, the group procured transportation into Gunnison and arrived with stories of a unique experience.[21]

During the summer of 1902, Marshall Pass provided one last look at the West characterized by Jesse James and Butch Cassidy. While Jesse James played havoc with the Missouri Pacific and Butch Cassidy's Wild Bunch caused alarm among the railroads in Utah and extreme western Colorado, the Marshall Pass section of the Rio Grande was the scene of a hold-up only once. Marshall Pass's lone experience with train robbers occurred on July 15, 1902, and was reported by the *Gunnison News-Champion*:

> *Monday morning the Denver and Rio Grande passenger train over Marshall Pass for Gunnison and the west was held up, the express car rifled, and the passengers relieved of their valuables. At ten minutes of nine the long train, filled with tourists and Colorado business men and women, was slowly winding down Marshall Pass near Mill Switch siding above Chester some eight miles below the pass and ten above Sargents. The engineer, John Ruland, noticed three men flagging the train. It is customary to pick up groups on the hill and the train slackened speed. Then he noticed that the men had guns in their hands and that a railroad tie was laid across the track with a boulder behind it. Not wishing to damage his train, Ruland brought it to a halt.*[22]

*A diamond-stacked 2-8-0 pauses on the summit siding on the east side of the pass. A snowshed covers the main track while the remarkably level eastern crest with its scattering of beaver ponds is visible in the background.*

COLORADO HISTORICAL SOCIETY

Once the passengers became aware of what was taking place, an air of hysteria gripped them as they quickly sought to devise all kinds of hiding places for their valuables. One hysterical young woman jumped into the lap of a rather portly gentleman, who, obviously pleased at the attention, consoled her by saying, "there, there, Miss, stay right here if it gives you any comfort." Many people hid money and valuables under the coach seats or tossed them along side of the roadbed. At gunpoint the fireman, Marion Myers, was sent through the cars telling everyone to get out and walk up the track. With the coaches clear, the robbers dynamited the safe in the express car and took its contents.[23] Then, after passing among the passengers and collecting their money and valuables, the robbers made a leisurely escape to the south. After their departure, the train reloaded and continued on to Gunnison with many of its passengers, most probably the ones who had lost the least money, quite thrilled at the adventure. At Sargent, a special was run back up the line to the scene of the hold-up to enable those who had hid valuables by the side of the track to recover them.

It is interesting to note that if the robbers had waited a day they would have made off with the Rio Grande's payroll for its employees on the western slope and the payrolls of many of the mining camps in the San Juans. These payrolls amounted to approximately $45,000, a far cry from the $1,500 taken. It would seem that the bandits were misinformed as to the date of the large shipment of money, for $1,500 was hardly worth the trouble when divided among five men. Manager Herbert of the Rio Grande notified Colorado Governor James Orman of the hold-up and asked him to request assistance from various law enforcement officials. Accordingly, Orman sent the following telegram to the sheriffs of surrounding counties: "Denver and Rio Grande passenger train no. 315 was held up and passengers robbed by four masked men two miles east of Chester station, west of Marshall Pass at 8:50 this morning. Use every effort possible to apprehend and arrest the robbers."[24]

A posse from Gunnison started on the trail of the outlaws, but lost the trail when a bloodhound became ill after a couple of miles; it was believed that the illness was caused by some type of poison left by the robbers to cover their trail. Many local residents believed there was something peculiar about the entire hold-up. As one citizen put it, "they never caught the culprits, but a district attorney later told me that he knew one of them. Said he was now a

*By 1898, the brick section house, lookout tower, and snowsheds over the summit turntable gave the feeling of permanence to the Marshall Pass operations. The tower looked down on most of the sixteen miles of track between the summit and Sargent, although there were many wintry days when nothing could be seen but blowing snow.*

DENVER PUBLIC LIBRARY - WESTERN HISTORY DEPARTMENT

# Denver & Rio Grande Railroad.

## Denver and Grand Junction.

(Read down)     Narrow Gauge.     (Read up)

In effect July 1, 1907

| *315 | Miles | STATIONS | *316 |
|---|---|---|---|
| 9 15 | 0.0 | Lv......Denver......Ar | 7 40 |
| 11 15 | 52.1 | Ar } ......Palmer Lake...... { Lv | 6 00 |
| 11 15 | | Lv } { Ar | 5 50 |
| 11 53 | 74.8 | Ar } ......Colorado Springs...... { Lv | 4 48 |
| 12 00 | | Lv } { Ar | 4 40 |
| 1 10 | 119.3 | Ar } ......Pueblo...... { Lv | 3 15 |
| 1 25 | | Lv } { Ar | 3 00 |
| 2 36 | 151.9 | Ar } ......Florence...... { Lv | 1 55 |
| 2 36 | | Lv } { Ar | 1 55 |
| 2 53 | 160.0 | Ar } ......Canon City...... { Lv | 1 35 |
| 3 03 | | Lv } { Ar | 1 35 |
| 5 10 | 215.1 | Ar } ......Salida...... { Lv | 11 35 |
| 6 45 | | Lv } { Ar | 8 40 |
| 6 57 | 220.1 | ......Poncha Junction...... | 8 26 |
| 7 20 | 226.0 | ......Mears Junction...... | 8 00 |
| 8 30 | 240.7 | Ar } ......Marshall Pass...... { Lv | 7 00 |
| 8 40 | | Lv } { Ar | 6 50 |
| 9 35 | 257.2 | Ar } ......Sargent...... { Lv | 5 45 |
| 9 35 | | Lv } { Ar | 5 40 |
| f 9 45 | 265.4 | ......Crookton...... | f 5 20 |
| f10 02 | 269.4 | ......Doyle...... | f 5 10 |
| 10 29 | 276.8 | ......Parlin...... | 4 53 |
| 10 45 | 288.6 | Ar } ......Gunnison...... { Lv | 4 25 |
| 10 50 | | Lv } { Ar | 4 20 |
| f11 02 | 294.4 | ......Hierro...... | f 4 03 |
| f11 13 | 299.1 | ......Iola...... | f 3 49 |
| f11 35 | 307.1 | ......Cebolla...... | f 3 25 |
| 11 55 | 313.9 | ......Sapinero...... | 3 05 |
| 1 04 | 329.0 | ......Cimarron...... | 2 10 |
| 1 30 | 334.5 | ......Cerro Summit...... | 1 30 |
| f 2 05 | 341.2 | ......Cedar Creek...... | f12 50 |
| 2 43 | 351.5 | Ar } ......Montrose...... { Lv | 12 15 |
| 2 56 | | Lv } { Ar | 12 05 |
| 4 53 | 387.4 | ......Ouray...... | 10 00 |
| 3 44 | 372.8 | ......Delta...... | 11 00 |
| f 4 45 | 397.6 | ......Bridgeport...... | f 9 48 |
| 5 20 | 411.7 | ......Whitewater...... | 9 12 |
| f 5 35 | 417.2 | ......Unaweep...... | f 8 57 |
| 5 55 | 424.1 | Ar......Grand Junction......Lv | *8 40 |

### Ouray Branch.

(Read down)     (Read up)

| *367 | M | STATIONS | *368 |
|---|---|---|---|
| 2 56 | 351.5 | Lv......Montrose......Ar | 11 58 |
| 2 58 | 352.1 | ......Ouray Junction...... | 11 54 |
| f 3 18 | 359.5 | ......Uncompahgre...... | f11 37 |
| f 3 57 | 374.0 | ......Dallas...... | f10 55 |
| 4 15 | 377.0 | ......Ridgway Junction...... | 10 45 |
| f 4 25 | 380.0 | ......Piedmont...... | f10 25 |
| 4 53 | 387.4 | Ar......Ouray......Lv | 10 00 |

### Coal Creek Branch.

| *125 | M | STATIONS | *126 |
|---|---|---|---|
| 3 40 | 151.9 | Lv......Florence......Ar | 4 15 |
| 3 55 | 154.6 | Ar......Coal Creek......Lv | 4 00 |

### North Fork Branch.

(Read down)     (Read up)

| *377 | M | STATIONS | *378 |
|---|---|---|---|
| 3 50 | 372.8 | Lv......Delta......Ar | 10 45 |
| f 4 20 | 380.8 | ......Austin...... | f 10 05 |
| f 4 35 | 385.4 | ......Payne...... | f 9 45 |
| f 5 05 | 392.5 | ......Rogers Mesa...... | f 9 15 |
| 5 30 | 397.8 | ......Hotchkiss...... | 8 45 |
| 6 10 | 405.9 | ......Paonia...... | 8 10 |
| 6 55 | 415.2 | Ar......Somerset......Lv | 7 30 |

### Crested Butte Branch.

(Read down)     (Read up)

| †347 | M | STATIONS | †348 |
|---|---|---|---|
| 11 00 | 288.6 | Lv......Gunnison......Ar | 4 15 |
| f11 45 | 299.3 | ......Almont...... | f 3 15 |
| 12 15 | 304.7 | ......Jack's Cabin...... | f 2 45 |
| 1 25 | 316.2 | ......Crested Butte...... | 1 45 |

All A. M. time is given in light figures; all P. M. time in heavy figures. *Daily.
†Daily except Sunday.

*Passengers delighted in the labyrinthine twistings of the railroad through the "Shawano Loop" and its snowsheds. The summit on the horizon lies four railroad grade miles away.*
WILLIAM H. JACKSON PHOTO, COLORADO HISTORICAL SOCIETY

*Looking west from the summit of Marshall Pass during the peak of the route's activity, one can see the water tank and buildings at Shawano (just to the left of the bare tree trunk) and two series of snowsheds on the "Shawano Loop."*
COLORADO HISTORICAL SOCIETY

prominent citizen of Grand Junction and his wife a leading social-light [sic]. When I asked him why he never arrested the man, he gave me some patter about 'limitations' that I never really believed."[25] Thus, Marshall Pass's one link with the West of Jesse James remained unsolved.

It was ironic that several days after the curtain call of one era took place on Marshall Pass, the prologue to another occurred. The *Denver Times* of July 19, 1902, reported under the headlines of "Over Marshall Pass in an Auto," that Thomas Gist of Denver had successfully negotiated the pass in an automobile. As far as was known, this was the first time that such an event had occurred. Gist made the trip up a portion of the old toll road and a railroad access road from Poncha Creek, and returned to Salida the same way. According to Gist, he had little difficulty with the route and predicted that it would soon become a popular drive.[26]

A few years later, the Marshall Pass route got a boost in business from their old rival. After a history of problems with Alpine Tunnel, the Denver, South Park, and Pacific finally gave up the Gunnison traffic for good in 1910. This left the Rio Grande as the only railroad running into the Gunnison country and ended an era of rivalry between the two roads which had seen, in its lighthearted moments, races between the engineers of the two roads on the paralleling straightaways between Gunnison and Parlin, twelve miles to the east.

In 1880, an ex-president, U. S. Grant, rode across Marshall Pass in a Sanderson stage. On September 23, 1909, the President of the United States, William Howard Taft, came west over Marshall Pass. The occasion was the opening of the Gunnison Tunnel, an irrigation project of the Federal Reclamation Bureau which diverted water from the Gunnison River to the farmlands of the Uncompahgre Valley. Gunnison was in an uproar all month in anticipation of the

*From a half-mile west of Shawano on the way to Chester, the buildings and water tank are visible at the head of the valley. Above the station are the snowsheds leading to the summit. The Continental Divide runs along the distant ridge while Mount Ouray towers 13,971 feet on the eastern slope.*

COLORADO HISTORICAL SOCIETY

*One of the first passenger trains in Gunnison sits beside the new depot ready to depart for Marshall Pass. The tracks are not yet fully ballasted and the yards in the distance are still under construction. The Baldwin 2-8-0 is pulling two flat-roofed baggage cars and a pair of coaches.*
DENVER PUBLIC LIBRARY - WESTERN HISTORY DEPARTMENT

presidential visit and accompanying celebration. Accompanied by a bodyguard of Colorado sheriffs and civic dignitaries, the President boarded a narrow gauge special at Salida for the trip over the pass to the tunnel site. Although there was some joking speculation as to whether the narrow gauge equipment could handle Taft's famous build, a special chair was installed in a narrow gauge business car to accommodate the large presidential beam.[27]

The fall of 1909 was also alive with speculations of improvements on the pass. A party of surveyors was busy making surveys along the route and there was talk of broad-gauging the line from Salida to Montrose and building a tunnel at the crest of the pass. The line from Grand Junction to Montrose had been converted to broad gauge in 1906. This left the section from Salida to Montrose the only narrow gauge segment of Palmer's original transcontinental route still operating. The idea of a tunnel through Marshall Pass had come up as early as 1880, and while the issue

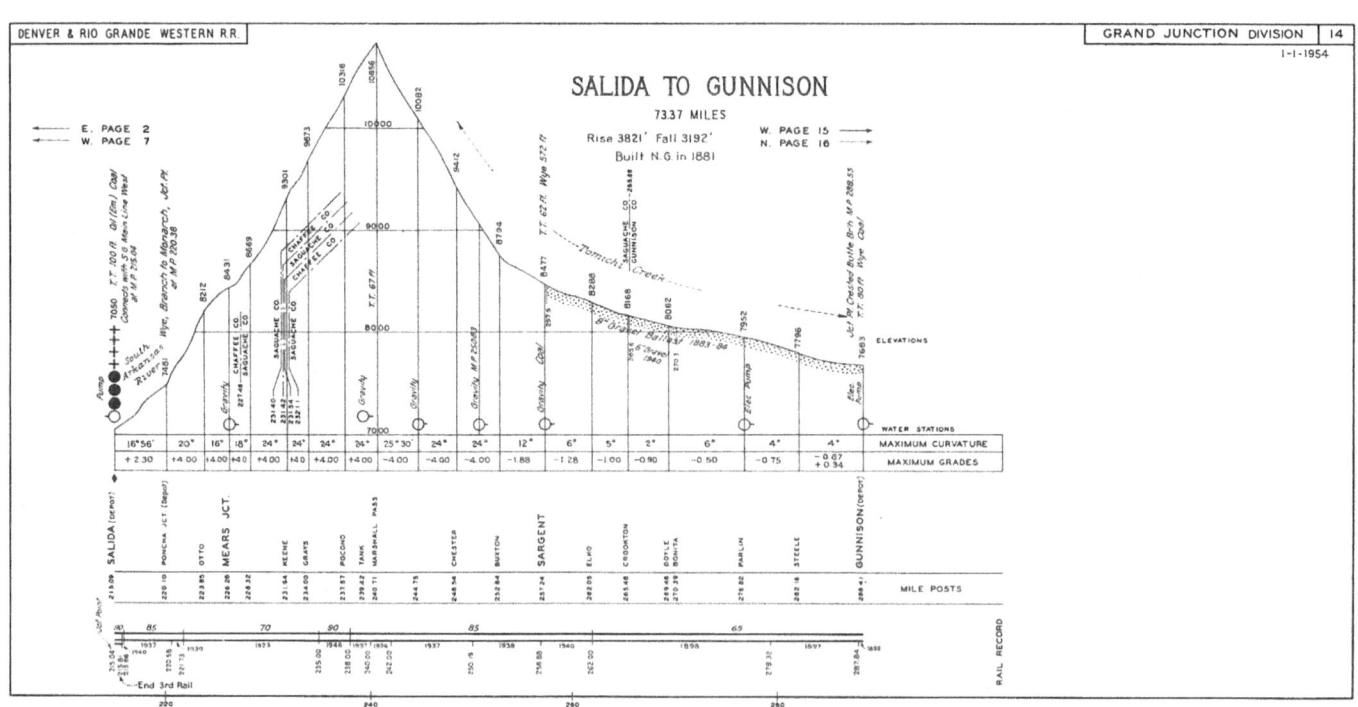

was raised again in 1909, there was little done about it. Two factors led to this decision. First, the Rio Grande was undoubtedly skeptical because of the South Park's failure with the Alpine Tunnel, although it must be noted that this did not stop the railroad on later projects, notably the Moffat Tunnel. Most importantly, the very geography of Marshall Pass would have demanded an extremely long tunnel. For example, building a tunnel from Shawano on the west to just below Pocono on the east would have lowered the elevation of the pass only 450 feet, but would have required a three-mile bore. Such a project was just not deemed feasible on a route whose existence and importance was even then in question. The idea of broad-gauging, however, was not so easily cast aside.

In September of 1912, President Benjamin F. Bush of the Denver and Rio Grande met with the Board of Directors in New York and decided to standard gauge the remaining 136 miles of narrow gauge between Salida and Montrose. The estimated cost for the broad-gauging was two million dollars. The *Gunnison News-Champion* reported that the decision was based on the need to accommodate the increasing transcontinental traffic, caused by the opening of the Western Pacific Railway, the Pacific coast extension of the Rio Grande. Also considered was the ever-increasing tonnage of fruit, coal, grain, cattle, and ore being produced on the Western Slope, particularly in the Gunnison and Uncompahgre Valleys. The directors were sure that having two standard gauge lines through the central Rockies would boost their business considerably. Naturally, Gunnison and the other towns along the Marshall Pass route were thrilled at the news.[28] Business along the pass had been decreasing steadily since the completion of the standard gauge over Tennessee Pass in 1890, and while the route did a satisfactory business in tourist trade and local traffic, the broad-gauging of the pass was sure to bring a much needed boost to the regional economy. Regrettably, the promises of broad-gauging were to remain unfulfilled.

When it became apparent to those along the route that the broad-gauging was just talk and would never come about, the death knell for Marshall Pass, which had sounded faintly in 1890, sounded again. While there is little doubt that a broad gauge line over Marshall Pass would have served the Rio Grande profitably well into the first half of the twentieth century, the railroad had some definite reasons for never undertaking the project. First, there was the railroad's own financial condition. With a corporate history of receiverships and near bankruptcies, the Rio Grande was far from a steady concern capable of pouring two million dollars into broad-gauging a

*Shawano nestled just 700 vertical feet below the summit of the pass, but the railroad required a four-mile loop to the north to gain the necessary elevation. Today, the Western Slope Gas Company pipeline goes directly from Shawano to the summit, which is the low point on the horizon.*
DENVER PUBLIC LIBRARY - WESTERN HISTORY DEPARTMENT

*In the days before half-tone photographs could be reproduced, pen-and-ink artists depicted the wonders of the West, often somewhat idealized, as is this sketch of the D&RG's Marshall Pass line. Needless to say, such drawings greatly excited the staid easterners.*
FROM RIO GRANDE, MAINLINE OF THE ROCKIES, BY LUCIUS BEEBE AND CHARLES CLEGG;
DOW HELMERS COLLECTION

section unless absolutely necessary. Thus, the key reason no action was taken, despite the initial decision of the Board of Directors, was that it was not absolutely feasible or necessary. While the *News-Champion* could justify its statements of September 20, 1912, with regard to the tonnage being developed in coal, fruit, cattle, and other products, there was no one industry that cried out for transportation as the mines had done around 1880. Likewise, with the Rio Grande's route over Tennessee Pass, there was no absolute demand for a through route between Denver and Salt Lake City. Thus, the action was temporarily postponed, and as time went on, only dust gathered on the idea.

When 1912 passed and no action was taken on broad gauging Marshall Pass, the future direction was clear. If 1890 was the zenith year in Marshall Pass history, then 1912 signaled the end of its prosperous years. From 1912 on, the trend was downhill with rapidly increasing speed. Although in 1912 the automobile was something that frightened horses and the airplane was something to stare at when at county fairs, they soon began to take their toll on the railroads.

In the years ahead, the automobile and airplane took from the railroad its passenger traffic and commerce, but they could not erase the close identification of the railroad with the land. Along Marshall Pass, as elsewhere in Colorado, the narrow gauge had become identified with every aspect of regional life and regional economy, and the memories of big men running little engines across a wilderness of natural elements became legendary. Long after the glory and fame were gone from the slopes of Marshall Pass, history would still recall that here had been a wooden railroad run by iron men.

---

[1] *Gunnison Daily News-Democrat*, August 17, 1881, p. 1.

[2] Athearn, *Rebel of the Rockies*, p. 122.

[3] *Gunnison Daily News-Democrat*, November 15, 1881, p. 4.

[4] *Ibid.*, November 15, 1881, p. 4.

[5] *Ibid.*, February 20, 1882, p. 1.

[6] Chappell, "Scenic Line of the World," p. 55.

[7] *Gunnison Review-Press*, July 5, 1884, p. 1.

[8] Chappell, "Scenic Line of the World," p. 55.

[9] *Gunnison Review-Press*, July 20, 1889, p. 2.

[10] Athearn, *Rebel of the Rockies*, p. 150.

[11] Dawson, "The Godfather of Marshall Pass," pp. 6-7.

[12] *Ibid.*, p. 8.

[13] George A. Crofutt, *Crofutt's Overland Tours* (Chicago: Arthur H. Day & Co., Publishers, 1888), p. 59.

[14] Ernest Ingersoll, *The Crest of the Continent: A Record of a Summer's Ramble in the Rocky Mountains and Beyond* (Glorieta, New Mexico: The Rio Grande Press, Inc., 1969), pp. 245-48. (Reprint of 1885 Edition).

[15] *Ibid.*, p. 249.

[16] Attributed to Rudyard Kipling. Original source unknown.

[17] *Harper's Weekly*, February 4, 1889, p. 79.

[18] *New York Times*, February 13, 1893, p. 3.

[19] *Gunnison Review-Press*, August 2, 1890, p. 1.

[20] Denver and Rio Grande Time-Table, Salida and Gunnison Routes, July 30, 1893.

[21] *Gunnison News-Champion*, December 29, 1938, pp. 1, 11.

[22] *Ibid.*, July 18, 1902, p. 1.

[23] *Ibid.*, p. 4.

[24] George G. Everett, *The Cavalcade of Railroads in Central Colorado* (Denver: Golden Bell Press, 1966), pp. 57-8.

[25] Betty Wallace, "Six Beans in the Wheel," Unpublished Master's Thesis, Western State College of Colorado, 1956, p. 104.

[26] *Denver Times*, July 19, 1902, p. 3.

[27] Lucius Beebe and Charles Clegg, *Narrow Gauge in the Rockies* (Berkeley: Howell-North, 1958), p. 69.

[28] *Gunnison News-Champion*, September 20, 1912, p. 1.

*Mears Junction was the key point on the eastern slope of Marshall Pass. Here, a mixed train has crossed the bridge over the Marshall Pass line and is doubling back past the station—climbing toward Poncha Pass.*

COLORADO HISTORICAL SOCIETY

# IV

# A Wooden Railroad Run By Iron Men

*No. 489 blots out the sun, working as a helper on Marshall Pass.*
ROBERT W. RICHARDSON PHOTO, DOW HELMERS COLLECTION

# IV |
# A Wooden Railroad Run By Iron Men

*"Much of the history of Colorado, at least its richest, its gutsiest, and most enchanting, has been written in its narrow gauge railroads."*
Lucius Beebe, railroad historian

*"I would go back tomorrow and do it all over again if I could."*
Oz Cooley, an engineer with the Rio Grande<br>for more than thirty-five years

*"I've seen the sunrise on Marshall Pass more times than anyone else."*
Merle Gregg, forty-nine year veteran<br>of the Rio Grande over Marshall Pass

*"Empires are the dreams of dreamers come true by the toil of common men."*
Walter R. Borneman

---

Few eras out of the American past can lend the excitement and adventure of small, black engines belching even blacker smoke as they fought their way westward to match the mountains and tame the land beyond. Likewise, few occupations captured the American imagination as did that of the locomotive engineer. In the late 1800s and early 1900s, the engineer was the legendary hero of American folklore, unequalled until an unknown young man named Lindbergh flew the Atlantic Ocean and turned the world's thoughts to something called an airplane. Nothing seemed to equal the fascination of songs about Casey Jones at the throttle of the *Cannonball Express*, or going down to Dixie on the *Wabash Cannonball*, or making up for lost time on the Old 97. William Jackson Palmer ran the Denver and Rio Grande, and Collis Huntington's name was synonymous with the Southern Pacific, but each depended on a breed of iron men who battled a host of natural elements to "get 'er there on time." Because of its high elevation, unpredictable weather, and treacherous terrain, the history of Marshall Pass is an integral part of the legacy of the mountain railroaders.

Probably few writers have expressed mountain railroading more poignantly than H. W. Stevens in "Adventure on the High Iron."

> *When oldtimers gather in the round house, the caboose, or even in the front office, the air grows thick with yarns which might hint at Paul Bunyan to an outsider. But these are no tall tales—railroading's past has high adventure and glamour in plenty without need of embroidery. And bright in the legends of the rails are the men who took 'er round the mountains and lived to tell about it. In the Rockies and the Appalachians, and in many an unnamed sawtooth range in the West and South, they fought gravity and worse with only the half-support of their primitive locomotives and brakes. But they were a tough breed, and kept a hand on the throttle always, lest Death reach out for it. For the mountain railroaders, danger lurked at every turn and frowning canyon slope. It could be death on the downgrade with runaway cars pushing violently from*

*behind, or death from the boulders hurtling down from above. It could come on some flaming trestle, or in the white rumble of an avalanche. It could come when a dog-tired dispatcher slipped up on orders, and a train plunging downhill met head-on with one panting up the grade.* [1]

It was no small coincidence that fatalities among mountain railroaders were high and that anxious wives kept glancing at the clock and straining to hear that familiar whistle when it came time. Marshall Pass boasted a host of dangerous, natural elements in steep curves, avalanches, high elevation, fierce winds, snow, and chilling cold. It took brave men to crawl gingerly along the top of a weaving boxcar setting the hand brakes in a driving, below zero gale which dropped the chill factor to an almost unbelievable depth. Nor was there any comfort in the locomotive cab. On wintry nights the fireman was faced first with the icy daggers of cold as he shoveled the coal from the tender and then was suddenly confronted with blinding heat as he tossed his load into the firebox. Neither was there any comfort for the engineer, a big man cramped in the little, narrow cab trying fruitlessly to scan the track ahead through whirling snow to see if an avalanche or rockslide had blocked the way. The stories of these railroaders which follow should make it clear that here, indeed, were iron men.

Like any railroad, the Denver and Rio Grande had to contend with the ever present possibility of train wrecks. Normally dangerous railroad equipment became even more dangerous when subjected to the twistings and windings of the road over Marshall Pass. The terrain, coupled

*Snow was a constant problem during the long winters on Marshall Pass. The snowsheds, wedge plow, and flanger all helped in the battle to keep the pass open, but it was the rotary plow that became the strong arm of the Rio Grande's winter warfare arsenal after 1889.*  COLORADO HISTORICAL SOCIETY

*Snow removal, wherever rails crossed passes in the high country, was expensive and was hard work, for both machines and men. The rotary pauses briefly, on the east side of Marshall Pass.*
COURTESY DONALD DUKE, GOLDEN WEST BOOKS: DOW HELMERS COLLECTION

with the difficulties of altitude, temperature, and snow presented an enormous challenge to the mountain railroaders. In recounting some of the wrecks on the pass it becomes vividly clear how hazardous it was to run a railroad through the mountains, and the horrible consequences that could occur because of a missed signal or loss of brakes. The first serious accident involving a passenger train on the pass occurred in May of 1882. A train consisting of a locomotive, mail car, two baggage cars, and two passenger coaches with sixty people on board was en route eastward from Gunnison when a mile west of the summit it suddenly careened to one side. Before the train could recover, every car turned completely over. Although few serious injuries occurred, the passengers were thrown violently from their seats. The most severely injured were two handcuffed prisoners from the Gunnison County Jail who were being taken to Pueblo.[2]

During the first decade of the railroad's operation over Marshall Pass, accidents were frequent; yet, they seem to have been less publicized than those of a decade or two later. One reason may have been their frequency. When a collision occurred between a hand car and train between Chester and Tank Seven on August 12, 1891, the Gunnison papers did not even report the incident. Three days later, on August 15, the *Gunnison Tribune* reported that "railroad accidents and fatalities are almost daily occurrences."[3] Indeed, it cannot be stressed enough that rockslides, mudslides, washouts, and avalanches created a constant peril along the pass. Countless accidents were never reported.

The *Mountain Mail* of Salida did report the hand car wreck. An eastbound extra pulled by No. 268 was laboring upgrade east of Tank Seven when it collided with a hand car coming down the hill with a section gang. Three men on the hand car were injured and taken to the Salida Hospital.[4] By coincidence, Engine 268 was to be the last of the C-16 class, 2-8-0 engines to be retired from service by the Rio Grande. Built by the Baldwin Locomotive Works in 1882, No.

268 and her sisters served as the back bone of the Rio Grande's motive force during the glory years of Marshall Pass before being gradually replaced by the heavier K-class 2-8-2's. Even then the 268 and many of her class continued to serve as helper engines and switching engines. Not until May of 1955, after three quarters of a century under steam, did the 268 retire to a permanent display in Gunnison.

Not all Rio Grande equipment was as faithful as the 268, and more than once air brakes failed and trains went rushing down the pass out of control as brakemen worked feverishly to set the hand brakes. At 1:30 on the morning of November 20, 1900, train No. 70, loaded with coal and coke from Crested Butte left the summit of the pass heading east and was descending towards Grays Siding when the air brakes failed. The engineer, Paddy Ryan, tied down his whistle in an anguished plea for hand brakes. Because of the momentum of the train and a covering of frost on the rails, the hand brakes had little effect and the train, with the exception of one car and the caboose, piled up on a sharp curve just above the section house at Grays Siding.

The conductor, Frank Perkins, was the only man able to move around, and in the wintry night he started down the track for Grays. Gilbert Lathrop in *Little Engines and Big Men* relates that the nearest telegraph station was at Shirley some six miles on down the track. Perkins commandeered a hand car at Grays and after forceful threats convinced the only occupant of the section house, an Italian who spoke little English, to go back to where the freight had wrecked

*Mears Junction, on the east side of Marshall Pass, also showing the San Luis extension and the mainline cross-over. Fifteen engines working steam, upgrade to Marshall and Poncha passes. From a watercolor painted by Mr. Henry Smith, one-time station agent at Mears Junction, circa 1885.*

ORIGINAL PAINTING IN SALIDA MUSEUM. DOW HELMERS COLLECTION

and flag the second section of the freight before it plowed into the caboose. Perkins then started down the valley for Shirley. Less than two miles from Grays, the hand car ran into a snow drift and stuck tight. Perkins could see the faint light of the Shirley station a thousand feet below him. Through the woods it was close to a mile to the station, while on the tracks it was almost four miles. Fearing he must act quickly to rescue his companions, Perkins plunged into the timber and waist deep snow. After much sliding, falling, and stumbling, he reached Shirley and telegraphed for doctors and a wrecker.

When the rescue party reached the wreck, they found a ghastly sight. The fireman, Bert Basswell, was buried beneath the mass of splintered cars, yet miraculously survived. Brakeman Charles Shaw was dead, and Engineer Paddy Ryan, suffering from internal injuries, died on the way to Salida. Two other brakemen were also seriously injured.[5] Perkins's dedication in going to Shirley undoubtedly saved their lives. It was acts like these which characterized the unselfishness of the mountain railroaders.

If some phantom engineer hooted past Perkins on his trek to Shirley it has gone unrecorded, but the isolation of the pass and its eerie setting on a wintry night made it a natural for legends and strange tales. One of the most interesting stories tells of a phantom train and an old engineer named Nelson Edwards. Edwards was a seasoned hand at the narrow gauge throttle and had never had a wreck when he came to Marshall Pass in the 1880s. For two months nothing eventful occurred. Then, one cold and frosty night as he peered out of the cab of his engine, it seemed to him that the silence was deeper than usual and the canyons darker. He had been

*Smoke escapes lazily through the snowshed cracks, as engine 483, pushing caboose 0585, emerges from sheds atop Marshall Pass.* MRS. W. R. THOMPSON PHOTO, DOW HELMERS COLLECTION

*Long westbound freight, consisting of "high" cars, waits while one of the powerful little 200s takes water at the Shirley tank, preparatory to helping the consist up the heavy grades to Marshall Pass. Note 3-way coupler.*
COURTESY JACKSON C. THODE, DOW HELMERS COLLECTION

warned about a defective rail and unsafe bridge and consequently scanned the track ahead with apprehension as he eased the train out of the summit snowshed.

Scarcely had Edwards left the snowshed when a whistle echoed through the mountains, and the gong in his cab signaled that the conductor wanted the train stopped. When asked by the conductor why he stopped, Edwards replied, "Because you gave the signal." The conductor said that he had done no such thing and told the engineer to "pull her open and hurry. We've got to pass Number 19 at the switches and there's a wild train behind us!" Edwards accordingly opened the throttle and moved down the grade.

Behind him the whistles came closer and closer, and, when he rounded a curve, Edwards looked back and saw a train rushing at full speed toward him. He opened the throttle full and his fireman heaped on the coal, but still the other train continued to gain. Through the snow Edwards saw the engineer of the pursuing train give a haunting laugh. Then, ahead of him he saw a lantern telling him to stop, and he took a chance and did so.

Behind him, the runaway train seemed about ready to leap on his train when it rolled off the tracks and crashed into the canyon. There were no sounds of agony—only silence. On the track in front of Edwards, the red lantern had disappeared, so the engineer continued down the grade and passed Number 19 at the switches without further incident. The next morning when he finished his run, Edwards found a warning written in frost on his cab window which read, "If you ever run here again, you'll be wrecked." No sign was ever found of the phantom train, but Edwards never ran over Marshall Pass again, going to work for the Union Pacific instead.[6]

*On December 11, 1892, a raging fire destroyed the round house and shop at Salida, Colorado. The fire started at 5:15 A. M. from oily waste in the cab of engine 419. A total of 17 engines were burned, with an estimated loss to the D&RG of $400,000.*
COURTESY MRS. W. R. THOMPSON, DOW HELMERS COLLECTION

It was only natural that such tales as this should spread, particularly when real events were not far from legend. Take for example, the case of Starr Nelson. In February of 1903, Dave Gast was taking a train of thirty-six empty coal cars west over the pass with two helper engines helping him along. At the top of the pass the helpers cut loose and started down grade for Sargent in front of Gast's train. Starr Nelson was at the throttle of the second helper and as he rolled along he thought he heard Gast behind him signal for brakes. As they rounded a curve Nelson again heard the shrill whistle and looking back saw Gast's runaway train speeding toward him. Nelson's fireman, Ed Davis, got down on the step and said, "Starr, I'm going to jump." The engineer looked at the boulder strewn hill side below and the hard bank of snow above and asked, "Where to?" Davis climbed back into the cab and watched Gast's train come closer and closer.

By now both engines were jumping on the rails, but Nelson figured if he could get to the next siding he could get out of the way. He made it to the siding and sent a streak of fire thirty feet into the air as he hit the brakes and skidded to a stop. Gast was not so lucky. His train plowed off the hillside and scattered empty coal cars all over the place. Gast had straddled a padded armrest and saved his life, but his fireman, Harry Goldwater, was crushed beneath the engine. The conductor had cut the caboose loose from the train and stopped it with hand brakes to save his life, but the front brakeman, Nelson Van Pelt, was also caught beneath the train and crushed.[7] Once more the iron and steel had demanded their dues.

A word must be said about the helper engines which worked Marshall Pass from Sargent and Mears Junction. Depending on their tonnage, trains were assigned a certain number of helper engines on each side of the pass. Adding one or two helpers was usually sufficient to boost a passenger train or empty freight over the Divide, but the heavier freights were often broken into sections for the thirty-mile run between Mears Junction and Sargent. Once the train reached the summit, the helpers were disconnected and either dispatched back down to their starting

*Engine 489 churning upgrade, slows down at the exact spot at Shawano where engine 451 blew up in September, 1923.*
ROBERT W. RICHARDSON PHOTO, DOW HELMERS COLLECTION

point or down the other side of the pass in front of the train, depending on where they were needed. Often, a freight would have the regular engine and a helper pulling in double-header fashion, with another helper pushing in the rear of the train. All signals passed between the engineers were blown by whistle, and it took a great deal of team work to coordinate speed and movements. The helper engines and the men who ran them were the unsung heroes of Marshall Pass. Often, they were stuck with irregular and tiring schedules. A crew might leave Sargent one morning fully expecting to return for supper that evening when a change of plans would put it in Salida instead. Helper engines and the men who ran them played an important role in the run over Marshall Pass just as they did on other mountain roads.

On July 25, 1901, the *Gunnison Republican* reported an accident on Marshall Pass and noted that it was the first wreck that had occurred on the pass for some time. It is difficult to know just what the *Republican*'s editor meant by "some time," but knowing the history of the pass, it is safe to assume that he was talking in terms of months or perhaps even weeks. In that wreck, a Pullman sleeper left the track a mile west of the summit snowshed, and rolled down the embankment. The car contained thirty passengers, and while all were injured, no one was killed.[8] Rail accidents were decreasing as the twentieth century began, but they were far from a passing phenomenon.

While mechanical failures on the trains, such as faulty air brakes, caused many wrecks, poor conditions on the road bed also accounted for quite a number. The nature of the land, with frequent rockslides and avalanches, particularly in the spring of the year, made keeping the track clear a nightmare. No less a problem was the extreme temperature to which the rails and roadbed were subjected. While the freezing and thawing of the ground might upset the curvature and bank of the roadbed unexpectedly, Gilbert Lathrop in *Little Engines and Big Men* described a mishap that occurred after certain curves on Marshall Pass were changed by men.

In December of 1915, Henry U. Mudge, new president of the Rio Grande, was on the Western Slope making an inspection tour when he decided to run an experiment on how fast the route from Montrose to Salida could be run. His engineer was a real "fireballer" named Tom Reardon, who had been working the Black Canyon run and had not been east over Marshall Pass for some time. By the time the special carrying Mudge reached Gunnison, Reardon had

*Near the turn of the century, a freight pauses at Shirley.*   DOW HELMERS COLLECTION

*D.&R.G. #402, the "Shoshone," was one of the big C-19s ordered for Marshall Pass service. Here, the engine pauses at the Shawano Tank with a short freight which includes two different versions of the Rio Grande's refrigerator cars for fruit and perishables.*   DENVER PUBLIC LIBRARY - WESTERN HISTORY DEPARTMENT

broken all existing records. Tom flew off the thirty miles to Sargent in forty-five minutes and hooked up with a helper engine for the climb to the summit of the pass. More records were set as Reardon reached the summit, unhooked the helper, checked the brakes, and whistled off down the east side.

Unfortunately, the year before, high officials in the general offices of the Rio Grande decided that the reason more tonnage could not be handled by one locomotive on the pass was that at slow speeds the wheels of the cars were binding on the inside rails. Consequently, the officials ordered the elevation removed from the curves. When Reardon came steaming down grade expecting to find elevated curves to speed around, he hit the levelled curves and Mudge's special went flying off the track. No one was seriously hurt and, according to Lathrop, even Mudge took the incident in good humor.[9] The train was not seriously damaged and a wrecker from the Salida yards soon had Mudge's special back on the track. Mudge continued with his inspection, but without any other races with time.[10]

Reardon was not the only west-ender from the Black Canyon run to have trouble on Marshall Pass. The main line west of Gunnison was still laid with thirty-five pound rails while much of the Marshall Pass line had been converted to fifty-pound. Long operation on the west end on the smaller rails caused the engines to develop grooves in their tires just the width of the steel. Thus, when an engine was finally run east over Marshall Pass for some reason, it could not find the traction to hold the rails on the wider steel. Because of the groove, only about one inch of the wheels actually touched on the face of the wider rail.[11] As if the railroaders did not have enough trouble, here was another item they had to worry about.

Death came to Marshall Pass again in December of 1909. Defective air brakes was the cause of an eastbound extra freight going out of control just as it left the summit snowshed. The freight rushed a mile down the east side of the pass out of control before the engine and a dozen freight cars left the rails. The engineer, Frank Parlin, was killed, and while the *News-Champion* also reported the death of fireman O. D. Cooley, he survived to work on the Rio Grande until the 1950s. Conductor Bill Jordan hiked back up the grade to the summit station and reported the wreck, while Brakeman Leslie Kerndt set up flares and lanterns to warn a scheduled passenger train of the danger. Because of the bitterly cold night, it was thought that the temperature had something to do with the failure of the brakes. The night was so cold that one of Kerndt's signal lanterns froze.[12] Kerndt went on to work for the Rio Grande for thirty-six years and retired with a healthy respect for the dangers of mountain railroading. Others were not so lucky.

Tom Dobbie started with the Rio Grande in 1887 and had been an engineer since 1898 when he sat at the throttle of No. 451 on Sunday evening, September 2, 1923. No. 451 was the lead engine of an eastbound freight that had just taken on water at Shawano. Dobbie eased the 451 about a quarter of a mile up grade from Shawano when the boiler exploded, sending scalding water and metal in all directions. Trainmen concluded that the explosion was caused by a faulty water gauge which had allowed Dobbie to misread the actual water level in filling the boiler at Shawano. Dobbie, a veteran of thirty-six years, and his fireman, E. E. Lindsey, a rookie of six weeks, were both killed.[13] Death it seemed, knew no discrimination. As so often was the case with train fatalities, both men left a number of grieving relatives and friends.

With such high fatality rates among the mountain railroaders, it was only natural that the old time religion of the mountains would give rise to appropriate hymns. Many a railroader was laid to rest after his last run to the hymn "Life Is Like a Mountain Railroad." It urged those

*Because of its four percent grade and sharp curves, Marshall Pass was the scene of many derailments and wrecks. This accident occurred on one of the curves between Grays Siding and Shirley. Notice the trucks on the embankment near the box car.*

COLLECTION OF GLENN GEORGE

*Tragedy struck near Mears Junction on August 6, 1935, and resulted in five deaths when a brake failure caused this pile-up.*　　LACY HUMBEUTEL PHOTO, DOW HELMERS COLLECTION

who were of good faith to "watch the hills, the curves, and tunnels, never falter, never fail, keep your hand upon the throttle and your eye upon the rail."[14] The men who ran over Marshall Pass never faltered and when they did fail, it was more from unsurmountable adversity, rather than human weakness. It was challenge enough that these men of iron were faced with danger from the mechanical elements of the trains they ran over the pass, but added to this was an element they could exercise no control over whatsoever—weather.

Despite man's technological advances, he has never been able to control weather; and, consequently, it has played havoc with many of his plans. Before the coming of the iron horse to the Rockies, winter was a time for the mountain man and freighter to head for lower country and wait for a renewal of life with spring. Even as William Marshall fought his way across Marshall Pass late in November, he was pressing his luck. Freak blizzards accompanied by fierce winds could deposit inches of snow within hours, blotting out all traces of trail and sign. With the settlement of the land and the coming of a population that did not pack up and head to lower country as the aspens turned, it became necessary to face the fury of Rocky Mountain winters head on. Few institutions battled the elements of winter with as much success and as many innovations as did the mountain railroads.

Before the railroad came to Marshall Pass, the freighters experienced many problems traversing the pass on skis, snowshoes, and sleds. Then, as long as the snow was stable, it did not really matter whether there was one foot of snow below the trail or a dozen feet. However, the iron horse was firmly anchored to the land and thus the annual task of keeping the track and roadbed clear began. Several years after the Rio Grande's struggle to keep the pass open began, the *Mountain Mail* estimated that the absence of snow one winter on Marshall Pass alone would save the railroad $100,000.[15] A sizable figure even now, the $100,000 could not begin to cover the lives lost to snow. Marshall Pass provided some of the toughest winter railroading in the Rocky Mountains. While the South Park had its problems at the Alpine Tunnel, and David Moffat's Denver, Northwestern, and Pacific fought winter on the heights of Rollins Pass, no railroad from 1881 until well into the twentieth century could match the record of continual service which the Rio Grande established on Marshall Pass. For three quarters of a century, the Lathrops, Reardons, Warmans, and Templetons of the Rio Grande kept the pass open.

Fully realizing what they were in for, the Rio Grande began building snowsheds along the summit of Marshall Pass in October of 1881. Despite J. C. Myers's prediction of November of that year, the sheds were not sufficient to eliminate snow removal problems completely. One draw back to the sheds was that blowing and drifting snow accumulated at the entrances of the sheds. Plows were often ineffective at getting in such places, and the task of clearing the track fell to section crews with shovels. Throughout the next several years, snowsheds were added at places where drifting occurred. The grand climax of snowshed building came late in 1883 with the completion of a shed on the very summit to shelter most of the switches and sidings and to protect the deep cut at the crest from the drifting snow. The roof of the shed was placed on trusses of heavy timber from seventy to eighty feet long and was covered with thick metal sheeting and a tar and gravel roof.[16] By this time, twenty-three of the sheds, some up to one thousand feet in length had been constructed on the pass. Snow fences were also built along ridges that

*The common wedge plow left several inches of snow on the rails which the engines then packed down so firmly that the flanges on the wheels could not grip the rails. Thus, the flanger was introduced into the Rio Grande's winter warfare arsenal during the winter of 1885-86. Its blades were designed to scrape the top of the rails and between them to remove the snow left by the wedge plow.*

AUTHOR'S COLLECTION

were apt to drift and at the head of gullies where the wind piled up the snow. The most notable of the snow fences was constructed on a curve two miles above Shawano and two miles below the crest of the pass. Constructed of heavy timbers and metal sheeting, this structure was braced to withstand the strongest of winds. Portions of it still stand today.

Physical structures along the route were not enough to keep the pass clear, and often times the result was that men with snow shovels were the only means of clearing the track. The common joke circulating in the round houses of Gunnison and Salida during the early 1880s was that engineers and firemen on the Marshall Pass branch were hired for a week on a trial basis, and then, if they showed a proficiency in shoveling through snow drifts, they were given steady jobs.

The first machine to tackle the snow of Marshall Pass was the ordinary wedge plow. It was built like a great "V" with contours to facilitate pushing the snow off the tracks as far as possible. Unfortunately, that was all the wedge plow did and many times by the middle of winter the snow had been piled so high on each side of the track that there was no place left to push the snow. Thus, the great innovations which Colorado winters demanded of the railroads began to appear.

The common wedge plow left a few inches of snow on the rails. The engine wheels packed this snow down so hard that the weight of the engine rested on the snow and thus prevented the flanges of the wheels from catching on the rails. Snow was also left between the rails and alongside of them. In the winter of 1885-6, the Denver and Rio Grande put a new invention called the snow flanger to work on the pass to combat this problem. The flanger consisted of a modified flat car with a series of blades which dug the snow from between the tracks and on each side of the rails. Pulled behind the engine, the flanger is said to have done during 1885-6 what it had taken fifty men to do the previous year. Consequently, the *Gunnison Review-Press* speculated that the flanger had saved the Denver and Rio Grande over $100 per day during the winter on Marshall Pass alone.[17] The flanger weighed 25,450 pounds, twice the weight of a loaded coal car, and was loaded with lead to make it ride heavy on the rails and not be buffeted around by the snow.[18] The South Park went one step farther with its innovations and equipped their engines with the Priest Flanger. It was almost like an ordinary flanger except that it was equipped with ice knives that actually scraped the inside edge and the top of the rail. Because of this it had to be raised and lowered by air at all sidings and switches.[19]

The flanger did nicely when the snow was only a foot deep or the rails needed cleaning, but it was no match for the deep drifts that the winds whipped up along the pass. Consequently, in 1889, the first rotary plows made their entrance into the Rio Grande's arsenal of winter warfare. Mounted on the front of the engine like the wedge plow, the rotary resembled a large, many-bladed fan which cut through the drifts and deposited the snow off to the side of the roadbed. Unfortunately, while the rotary was successful with drifts, it did not do so well with slides and avalanches. Slides usually contain rock and debris which raised havoc with the rotary blades, thus summoning the reliable section hand with shovel to clear the way for the machine. Still, the rotaries were so successful that when several snowsheds on Marshall Pass burned in the summer of 1889, they were not rebuilt because of the new snow removers's effectiveness.

By 1889, only eighteen of the original twenty-three snowsheds were still standing on the pass, and it became understood that in the event other sheds were destroyed they would not be replaced. This brought a cry of relief from passengers and tourists who travelled the route and were annoyed because the coaches filled with smoke during their passage through the sheds. The *Review-Press* asserted that "the trip over the hill will be much more pleasanter [sic] without these sheds, as the cars are more or less filled with smoke while passing through them, and besides the view is obstructed at some of the prettiest portions of the road. The snowshed must go."[20]

The Rio Grande would have gladly obliged the *Review-Press*, but the wintry weather of the pass would not permit the destruction of all the sheds. One further innovation came out of the mountain railroading of Colorado. More prevalent on the South Park than the Rio Grande, the Jull plow came to battle the snow in 1890. Named for its inventor, Orange Jull, the Jull plow was similar to the rotary, but employed a huge auger device which bored through the snow and then discharged it either to the right or left of the track. The Jull's try for glory came in competitive trials with the rotary in April of 1890 near Hancock on the South Park line east of the Alpine Tunnel. With many side bets and much commotion, the two plows, each with three engines attached, took turns running up grade through the drifts until they were stopped. For two days the contest was a draw, but on the third day a flaw was found in the Jull. The Jull plow worked fine in hard-packed snow, but in loose snow instead of boring through, the auger only pushed the snow ahead of it; finally the snow would pile up and cover the plow, stalling it. Thus, the rotary emerged victorious and the Jull went back to its designers.[21]

Even with such inventions as the flanger and rotary plow, the Rio Grande still had problems during the winter on Marshall Pass. On one particularly bitter winter day in 1919, the dispatcher at Sargent could plainly see that a storm was raging on the crest of the Divide. He decided to couple three engines onto a flanger and send them to assist a double-headed passenger train over the pass to Salida. The five engines labored up the grade until they came to a long snowshed about a mile below the summit of the pass. The first two engines plunged into the shed and came to a jolting stop. The shed was filled almost to the roof with wind-packed snow and ice. The other three engines tried without success to pull the two engines out of the shed, but they were stuck tight. When it was obvious that they could not be freed, the conductor started wading through the drifts to the summit to get help, while the remaining three engines backed the passenger train back down the grade out of the worst of the storm.

While the crews of the two marooned engines fought the bitter cold, the conductor reached the top and sent instructions for a rotary plow to break through the drifts and free the engines. However, even the rotary had a tough time getting through the drifts and it was almost twenty-four hours after the engines first shuddered to a stop in the shed that help finally came. As the rotary neared the shed, the noise became deafening and echoed through the shed so that it seemed twice as close as it actually was. After spending a numbing night in below zero weather, the crews were sure that they would be rammed by the rotary. But the plow stopped well clear of the engines, and section hands shoveled out the two engines. While the two engines returned to Sargent, the plow continued to open the pass for the passenger train which had been delayed almost twenty-four hours.[22] The years of the twentieth century may have heralded some remarkable achievements, but Mother Nature still ruled the heights of Marshall Pass.

Although the Alpine Tunnel may have gotten more publicity for bad weather, and the crews of the South Park may have been called the "snowbuckingest fools" in the world, Marshall Pass provided the Rio Grande with its share of snowbound stories. In December of 1884, a driving storm accompanied by fierce winds lashed the pass for six days during which no train crossed the Divide. Reports indicated that snow piled up to heights of five to ten feet with the winds building drifts even higher. Many of the snowsheds were drifted full and packed solid. Snowplows were of little use because the alternate thawing and freezing had turned the snow to ice, so the job had to be done by men and shovels. The wind was so ferocious that some of the snowsheds were damaged. Finally, on December 26, the storm let up and the crews drove through the pass, freeing stranded trains.[23]

Cy Warman, the poet laureate of the Rockies, got a taste of wintry conditions when he was sent out to clear Marshall Pass in 1887. Warman was ordered out to double-head an engine plowing on the pass. Ten miles above Sargent, he was side-tracked to await the plow which was working somewhere between Shawano and the summit. As time passed and the plowing engine did not steam into the station, it became clear that it had become stuck somewhere on the hill. Warman had no plow on his engine, but set out to buck the drifts toward the stranded engine.

Unfortunately, the wind-swept drifts from eight to eighteen feet proved too much for Warman's engine and he too became hopelessly marooned. The devilry of the wind was brought into sharp focus by the drifts, which in places left only the very tops of the telegraph poles visible. It was a week before plows broke through to the summit and began freeing the stranded trains and Warman was once more under steam.[24] The pass was clear, but the men of iron drove their tiny engines knowing full well that it would only be a matter of time until snow fell again.

The battle to keep the pass open during the winter resulted in a quest to beat the unbeatable foe; yet, there seemed to be a strange drive to survive and prevail among the mountain railroaders. The railroad was on Marshall Pass, and snow or no snow, the men who operated over it understood that their job was to get the trains through. They knew it was dangerous, yet, equally so, there was a fire in them which made them love the smell of coal smoke and the pounding of drivers. The key to these men was that despite tremendous sacrifices life went on. Frank E. Gimlett, the Hermit of Arbor Villa, related a story which seems to focus the whole struggle of life on the pass. In the winter of 1885, Gimlett was on a train which was marooned on the pass between Shawano and the summit for four days. Fortunately, the baggage car contained bacon, eggs, oranges, and other foods, and the passengers set about preparing meals and taking turns sleeping in the bunks of the sleeper. On the second day, the group received a new member when a baby was born on the train; on the third day, Cy Beeler, an old prospector from White Pine,

*Rear brakeman's view of his train as it enters the Marshall Pass snowsheds, eastbound. The snow fences at lower right helped greatly to lessen snowdrift problems on this stretch.*

COURTESY LACY HUMBUETEL, DOW HELMERS COLLECTION

dropped off to his final rest. Thus, life had come and life had gone, but the world went on. With the arrival of the snowplows, the train made its way on into Gunnison with the passengers accepting the incident as just one of those things.[25]

Naturally, winter made for irregular train service over the pass and the irregular service made for some difficult times in Gunnison and the surrounding area, which depended on the goods that came in over the pass on the Rio Grande. Activity in the mining camps dropped to minimum levels during the winter and the miners had little to do but wait for the supplies brought to Gunnison and Crested Butte by the railroad. One winter, when an exceptionally hard snow closed Marshall Pass, Crested Butte had no train for twenty days. The story is told that when the food ran low in the coal camp, the miners just tightened their belts and cussed the Denver and Rio Grande. When, however, the word got around that there was only a three-day supply of whiskey and beer left in camp a hundred men took to their skis and went to shovel out the track to meet the train.

One of the most famous snowbound stories on Marshall Pass has the South Park playing a leading role. It has been said that while the Denver and Rio Grande may have been the biggest, the toughest, and the best of the mountain railroads, it could not match the charm and charisma of the South Park. Two South Park engineers demonstrated that charisma and the determination of the individual man during a wintry storm around the turn of the century. The storm had blocked Alpine Tunnel and caught South Park engineers Andy Nelson and Billy Kerns on the

*A rotary works up the east side of Marshall Pass. With full power from the locomotives, the forward speed at this point was less than four miles per hour.*

COURTESY DONALD DUKE, GOLDEN WEST BOOKS, DOW HELMERS COLLECTION

Gunnison side of the Divide far from their regular hangout at Como on the South Park line to Denver. The Alpine Tunnel was blocked so completely that there was little hope of opening that route until spring. Marshall Pass was also blocked, but because of its lower elevation, Nelson and Kerns figured the snow would not be as bad, and came up with the idea of opening Marshall Pass for the Rio Grande. The South Park would be glad to have its engines back, the Rio Grande would be happy to have the pass opened, and the two men would get back home. Rio Grande officials gave the two South Park engineers permission and clearance to try it, and on a Sunday afternoon with the temperature at forty degrees below zero, the engines steamed east out of Gunnison for the pass.

At Sargent, the thermometer dropped even lower, and after a hot dinner and some spirits to warm them up, the engineers started up the pass. They were told to keep an eye out for ten Rio Grande engines that were stalled at various points along the way. They found three of the engines still alive and coupled on to them for the push to the summit. About three-quarters of a mile from the top, Nelson and the No. 71 became uncoupled from the other engines and churned ahead. Because he was making headway, Nelson did not stop, but instead, plowed on through to the summit. Imagine the Marshall Pass operator's surprise when the first sign of activity he had seen in days turned out to be a lone South Park engine. The operator received orders to hold the South Park engines at the summit because two Rio Grande engines with a large wedge plow were working somewhere on the east side above Grays Siding. After waiting twenty-one hours in the snowshed on the summit, orders came for Nelson and Kerns to run light down the east slope and see what had happened. Four and a half miles from the summit they found the Rio Grande crews hopelessly stuck in the snow. They plowed to within several feet of the dead engines and then shoveled them out by hand. Farther down the pass Andy and Billy passed six more dead engines before steaming into Salida Tuesday morning after having opened Marshall Pass for the Rio Grande. A short time later, they were on their way north to Como and home.[26]

Weather conditions were not the only natural difficulties which faced the mountain railroaders of Marshall Pass. Much has been said about the difficulties imposed by the terrain of the pass, and the consequent need for bridges, steep cuts and fills, and an ever watchful eye for rock slides and cave-ins. What is not always thought of when one speaks of difficult terrain is the altitude above sea level. Not only was the Rio Grande faced with corkscrewing its road 2,400 feet up from Mears Junction to the summit, but they were also faced with the effects of an altitude of 10,846 feet on men and machinery once they reached the top. At two miles above sea level, the gradual thinning of the air causes mind and reflexes to become less keen, particularly when aided by the blistering heat of summer or the biting cold of winter.

Many of the men who worked on the railroads of Colorado had spent some time there getting adjusted to the altitude, but those who came in fresh from the East soon learned that it took a great deal more breath and stamina to run along the top of a swaying box car at 10,000 feet. Many were the tourists from the East whose awestruck stares at the scenery were interrupted by nosebleeds, dizziness, and that queasy feeling associated with altitude sickness. Indeed as Ernest Ingersoll observed, "it was a daring scheme to run the road over here,"[27] and likewise, it took men of stamina and vigorous health to keep it running.

In an era when European mountaineering was just reaching its glory, the nation and world watched anxiously as the mountain railroads of the Rockies battled for the altitude record. The Denver and Rio Grande established the first significant altitude record in the United States by crossing 9,383-foot Veta Pass in June of 1877. Two years later, in May of 1879, the Denver, South Park, and Pacific captured the title by building over 9,991-foot Kenosha Pass en route to the Alpine Tunnel and Gunnison. November of 1880 found the Rio Grande with the record again after completing its line over 11,330-foot Fremont Pass northeast of Leadville. Thirteen months later on December 21, 1881, the South Park snatched the title back by completing the Alpine

Tunnel to set the record at 11,612 feet at the apex of the tunnel. These altitude records were all set by narrow gauge railroads.

In the fall of 1887, the Colorado Midland en route from Leadville to Aspen, completed the standard gauge Hagerman Tunnel through the Continental Divide at an altitude of 11,528 feet. The Hagerman Tunnel held the altitude record after the Alpine Tunnel shut down between 1888 and 1895, although it was abandoned for the lower Busk Ivanhoe Tunnel (10,944 feet) in 1893. If there was a discrepancy in records between the narrow gauge South Park and the standard gauge Midland, David Moffatt's Denver, Northwestern, and Pacific firmly set the record for any gauge by crossing 11,680-foot Rollins Pass in 1904. Rollins Pass held the record until 1937 when, as a part of the Rio Grande system, it was abandoned for the Moffat Tunnel. The record then fell to the narrow gauge line across Marshall Pass with its elevation of 10,846 feet. When the Marshall Pass line was finally abandoned in 1955, the route which brought about its demise, the Rio Grande standard gauge over Tennessee Pass, captured the record with a crossing of

*On February 9, 1974, one hundred years and a few months after William Marshall's historic crossing, Omar Richardson, Dolora and Gary Koontz, and the author set out to ski the twelve miles to the summit of Marshall Pass from Sargent. The temperature on leaving Sargent at 6:30 A.M. was - 39°, a small indication of the bitterness of Marshall Pass's winters. Here, Richardson (with the author's ski poles) and Koontz pause at Shawano by the Western Slope Gas Company pipeline just prior to starting up the pipeline cut to the summit.*
AUTHOR'S COLLECTION

*With three to four feet of snow on the ground, skis are the only sane mode of transportation on Marshall Pass since the abandonment of the railroad. The skiers of the author's party reached a point half-way up the pipeline cut to the summit where the author broke a ski binding, forcing a prompt retreat down the twelve miles to Sargent. Their arrival at Sargent at 9:00 P.M. with the temperature again sinking to - 40 ° signaled the end of a very long day.*
AUTHOR'S COLLECTION

10,239 feet via the Tennessee Pass Tunnel.[28] The battle for the heights was won, but not without tremendous personal sacrifice.

Through mountainous terrain, fighting a host of natural elements, the mountain railroaders of Marshall Pass established a legacy of courage and self-sacrifice that stands among the finest in American railroading. Few places could match the physical difficulties of the pass, and even fewer could match the three-quarters of a century which saw locomotives pounding its grades. As the years of the railroad's glory over Marshall Pass drew to a close, and the history that would be its final chapter was acted out, the men who made that history probably would have chuckled if one had told them that they and the men before them would remain a part of American folklore forever. Perhaps in that chuckle is the meaning of iron men.

---

[1] H.W. Stevens, "Adventure on the High Iron," *Esquire* (October, 1946), p. 87.

[2] *Gunnison Daily Review-Press*, May 27, 1882, p. 5.

[3] *Gunnison Tribune*, August 15, 1891, p. 2.

[4] Everett, *Cavalcade of Railroads*, p. 99.

[5] Gilbert A. Lathrop, *Little Engines and Big Men* (Caldwell, Idaho: Caxton Printers, Ltd., 1954), pp. 80-82.

[6] Amanda Ellis, *Legends and Tales of the Rockies* (Colorado Springs: Denton Publishing Company, 1954 ), pp. 41-2.

[7] *Gunnison Tribune*, February 27, 1903, p. 1.

[8] *Gunnison Republican*, July 25, 1901, p. 1.

[9] Lathrop, *Little Engines and Big Men*, pp. 252-55.

[10] *Gunnison News-Champion*, December 17, 1915, p. 1.

[11] Lathrop, *Little Engines and Big Men*, pp. 217-18.

[12] *Gunnison News-Champion*, December 24, 1909, p. 1.

[13] *Ibid.*, September 7, 1923, p. 1.

[14] Chuck Willingham and Fred Bender, "Life Is Like A Mountain Railroad."

[15] *Mountain Mail*, December 25, 1885, p. 3.

[16] *Gunnison Daily Review-Press*, December 24, 1883, p. 3.

[17] *Gunnison Review-Press*, December 12, 1885, p. 6.

[18] Everett, *Cavalcade of Railroads*, p. 70.

[19] Poor, *Denver, South Park, and Pacific*, p. 318.

[20] *Gunnison Review-Press*, July 20, 1889, p. 2.

[21] Poor, *Denver, South Park, and Pacific*, p. 353.

[22] Everett, *Cavalcade of Railroads*, pp. 191-92.

[23] *Gunnison Review-Press*, December 27, 1884, p. 7.

[24] Cy Warman, *Tales of an Engineer* (New York: Charles Scribner's Sons, 1897), 81-85.

[25] The Hermit of Arbor Villa (Frank E. Gimlett), *Over Trails of Yesterday*, Vol. VII (Salida, Colorado: By the Author, 1948), pp. 40-41.

[26] Poor, *Denver, South Park, and Pacific*, p. 371.

[27] Ingersoll, *Crest of the Continent*, p. 245.

[28] Sprague, *The Great Gates*, p. 353.

*Engines 499 and 496 with caboose 0586 on the drawbar, created this spectacular picture at the bridge across Poncha Creek, between Otto and Mears Junction.* ROBERT W. RICHARDSON PHOTO, DOW HELMERS COLLECTION

# "There's Something about Railroading that a Man Enjoys"

*With a good fire and a full head of steam, engine 483 waits at Sargent to help the next eastbound train for Marshall Pass.*
LACY HUMBEUTEL PHOTO, DOW HELMERS COLLECTION

# V | "There's Something about Railroading that a Man Enjoys"

*IN THE LATE 1960s, DOW HELMERS INTERVIEWED RAILROADERS WHO HAD WORKED THE LINE OVER MARSHALL PASS. HIS RECOUNTING OF THEIR REMINISCENCES REAFFIRMS THEIR LEGACY OF IRON MEN.*

## SELECTED INTERVIEWS FROM THE DOW HELMERS COLLECTION

"When they wrecked, those little wooden cars demolished. They didn't try to pick them up—just burned them right there."
    Merle Gregg, forty-nine year veteran with the Rio Grande

"In winter, we would pull up at a water tank and by the time you got your tank filled with water, your hair, where you had been sweating, would be just icicles."
    William Crylie

"And it tossed me on the floor, and bumped my head, many, many a time. Yet we always laughed it off, because we loved the Rio Grande line. Now when you pull up a rail, or abandon even a short branch line, it tears at my heart strings to thus abuse an old friend of mine."
    Frank E. Gimlett, "The Hermit of Arbor Villa," from "Over the Trails of Yesterday, the Gold and Silver West."

*Ted McDowell, Salida, Colorado, Conductor on Marshall Pass.*
DOW HELMERS COLLECTION

"Once I was on the crew going west, there was another crew going east and the hill crew got in there (Marshall Pass summit) all at the same time. We had nine engines up there at one time. We had to do quite a bit of see-sawing to get all the trains by. Took us about twenty minutes to figure out how to do it, but we did!"
    Ted McDowell, Rio Grande engineer

"But who shall chronicle the ways
Of common folk, the nights and days
Spent with the rough goatherds on the snows,
And travelers come whence no man knows?"
    Rudyard Kipling

"Memory is a Rosary of Recall. It is a gracious necklace of the human spirit. Each bead is a past event or precious experience kept shining with the fadeless lustre of the mind."
    Hal Boyle

## Merle Gregg
### Poncha Springs, Colorado

"I worked for the Grande for forty-nine years. They finally pulled me out of service. You see, I was seventy years old. All that time was spent here in the valley—all on the Rio Grande. My wife was born right here, at Poncha. I was born in Kansas. I came to Pueblo when I was about four or five years old . My father was a general foreman on the zinc works. When we moved up here to Salida, we had a ranch down below Poncha. I was raised on the ranch and have been around here more than sixty years.

"When I started with the railroad it was as a fireman. When I first went to work, I worked in the shops, there at Salida, as a machinist's helper. I ran a big drill press there for a while, then me and the foreman disagreed so I went in to see Haskins, who was a master mechanic. I asked if he was hiring any firemen. He said, "Yes, what's the matter with the job you have?" I said, "I just quit." He said, "Go over to the hospital, get examined, and go to work." I said, "OK," and that was it.

"I went to work on the narrow gauge over Marshall—all on a scoop shovel, too. A run would be from Salida to Gunnison. We would shovel about eight or nine tons of coal from here to Gunnison. Coming back, we would have to take coal at Sargents then go to the top of the hill. We would set out half our train at Sargents and take all we could pull with three engines—nineteen cars. We would take them to Marshall Pass and set them out and then go back to Sargents, get another tank of coal, and go back up, put our train together and come to Salida. It was always

*Dow Helmers, August 27, 1967*  CHARLES WEBB PHOTO

*D&RGW #488 at Salida, Colo., in 1927.*  R.H. Kindig, Dow Helmers Collection

around fourteen to sixteen hours on a trip when we doubled the hill. We shoveled about (I think they held around nine tons) eighteen to twenty tons of coal, and that's a lot of shoveling! A lot of times we would stop at the bridge right there at the depot after sixteen hours, and I would have to take a broom and sweep up what coal I could and put it in to keep the engine hot—alive—until somebody, a hostler, could take over.

"They wouldn't promote us fellows because it was so hard to get firemen who could fire those little engines and we should have been promoted years before we were. In our class of engine the cab set over the top of the boiler—on each side of the boiler. The boiler was between you and the engineer. When firing, you had to get down between the tender and the fire box. When you got up Marshall Pass you stood right there from the time you started till you got to the top of the hill. In those little engines you just had to stand there, watch your steam gauge and put in two or three scoops of coal all the way, you never sat down.

"One time we left Salida and we got up as far as Grays Siding. We had three engines and we were there when the 315 left Salida about six o'clock in the morning and we were still at Grays when they got there. They had a flanger with two engines ahead of them and they had two engines on the passenger, I think, of about five coaches. They took our three engines off our train and coupled us all together to get from Grays Siding to Marshall Pass with the passenger train —that added up to seven engines and five coaches! The passenger train then made it downhill all right. Of course, the flanger went on down ahead of him, while we came on back to our train. It was all clear then and we took our train to Marshall Pass without further trouble.

"We always had more freight eastbound than westbound. We always had loads coming this way. I have seen three, four, and five sections of stock trains eastbound out of Gunnison, one behind the other.

"We ate at Mrs. Hendricks's eating house at Sargents all the time. We always ate coming east, because by the time we cleaned a tank of coal from Gunnison to Sargents we were all ready to eat. She sure put out a good meal. Fifty cents for all you wanted. Now you couldn't get that for $5.00!

"One time going up Marshall Pass, I was firing for a fellow named Luke Daly. He was an awfully nice guy—I fired for him a lot. But the minute we would hit the hill up there where we were down to about five or six miles per hour with those heavy trains, he'd cock his feet up and go to sleep. I'd work the injector and work the sand for him and let him sleep. When we got up above Shirley and around the big curve, I slipped out, took the red lantern, and set it on the running board right in front of him. We had orders to meet a train at Grays Siding and when we came around a curve, the helper was sitting on the siding. I shouted, 'By God, Luke, there they are!' He reared up and saw that red light and he cleaned the clock shoving the engine into reverse. We tore up the train and jerked out a drawbar. The rear engine like to went through the caboose and pushed it across ways on the track. We spent the rest of the night trying to get that train back together, but he didn't dare tell on me."

## Margaret Hendricks
### Salida, Colorado

"There was a roundhouse at Sargents when I first came there. Usually there were at least nine or ten engines and ten or eleven crews stationed at Sargents. These were helpers to take the loaded trains eastbound up the steep grades of the pass. When they tore that roundhouse down, I got some of the big windows and used them on the sun porch of my home.

"There was no place to eat in Sargents, so the crews, over from Salida, brought their lunches. But if they got held up for any reason, they were out of luck. I knew most of the men and their families, from having lived in Salida. One day a couple of the men who I knew quite well, came over and asked me if I could feed a couple of crews. I told them that I thought I could and they beat it off to the store to get everything I needed. About a dozen hungry men showed up. From then on, whenever they came to town, they asked me to feed them. Later, they installed some sort of a telephone in my house. The phone didn't ring, it would 'whoooo.' With this they would call me from the top of Marshall Pass and tell me how many would be there and about what time. Sometimes I had only about forty-five minutes to rustle up a meal for eight to ten men. Eastbound crews would call me from Doyleville. The men were all so jolly and gentlemanly, I enjoyed serving them and did it for quite a while.

"Once a coal train got away. While the crews were busy with something else, and before the helper engine was coupled, the train started drifting out of the yard. It rolled free down to a place called Elko Siding, where several of the coal cars left the tracks and turned over. The ranchers picked up much of this coal, but later a railroad detective appeared and made them pay for the coal at $15.00 a ton.

"Several years after I started cooking, Miss Ora Rising established a regular eating house for railroaders. There was once a hotel, down at the end of the street. For many, many years there was a big timber company at Sargents. They had a big mill and they produced telegraph poles.

"There was never a law officer in Sargents. Oh, for a few years Harvey Hicks was Justice of the Peace, but I can't recall of his ever trying a case. Sargents was just simply a grand place to live!"

## FRANK VEO
## SALIDA, COLORADO

*Frank Veo started with the Rio Grande in 1906 at the age of thirteen as a caller [a messenger whose job it was to summon trainmen for their shifts] in Leadville. Three years later, he started firing engines on the Marshall Pass route and was promoted to engineer during World War I.*

"At one time it was said if you didn't work for the railroad, you didn't live here—used to be that.

"Trainmen didn't like to ride in the caboose with one of them big helper engines shoving against it—something could happen and the engine would go right through them.

"Running time from Marshall Pass to Sargents and from Marshall Pass to Poncha Junction was 12 mph and if we got over 12 mph we began to kinda sweat. You could check your speed by mile posts or after you'd worked for awhile you could tell by looking at the ground.

"It's four miles from Marshall Pass down to Shawano by going around the track, but you can go up that draw afoot and it only is about a half mile.

*Frank Veo, retired engineer, Marshall Pass.*
DOW HELMERS COLLECTION

*Engine 486, almost engulfed in snow, pauses at Sargent, just down from Marshall Pass, in 1952, with Frank Veo, longtime engineer on the 3rd Division, leaning out the right side of the cab.*
COURTESY MRS. W. R. THOMPSON, DOW HELMERS COLLECTION

Lots of times we'd drop off the engine and we'd go up the draw and when they'd come by after awhile we'd get on again.

"You could feel the air when you left the pass. When the car man got done with you, there was air in the auxiliary reservoirs under the cars, but the pistons that shoved the brakes up against the wheels, there wasn't any air behind them. When you topped out, you made a ten or fifteen pound reduction of air and if you didn't get some action and feel that train you didn't have it, so the best thing you could do then was to get off. It was experience that taught you. The engineer commanded the air. The fireman slept going down the hill—the engineer slept coming up the hill."

## Gus Latham
### Marshall Pass, Colorado

*A bit of a "tingle" ran up my spine when a voice called "Come in." I was about to meet and talk with a man who had spent much of his adult life on the pass . . . Gus Latham, former railroader and erstwhile U.S. Postmaster of Marshall Pass (population 11) greeted me warmly and quickly made me feel at home.*

"When I started with the Grande we worked ten hours a day. Later this was cut to eight. I was at Tank 7 three years, then I moved to Marshall Pass when they had an opening. That was in 1930. I was a section man. They had a double section, going both ways. The sections were four miles long and six men comprised a section crew. The trains constantly spread the rails on those 24° curves and we would re-align them. We would curve those little rails by man-strength and bars, first nailing down a few feet, then spring the rails a nail along as we went. We didn't actually bend the iron, just sprung it. We used an iron track gauge, which measured three feet inside the rails.

"When I first went to Marshall Pass they had a Post Office there and the agent, of which there were three, one for each of the three shifts, was the Postmaster. But when they began to cut things down in 1940, they didn't have any Postmaster so the men that were there made the proposition that I be postmaster, which was an after-supper job of only an hour or so. During the daytime I continued to work for the railroad.

"I got with the Postmasters in Denver and attended the state conventions; then it came time for an annual convention in New York (October 19, 1948) and I went. The *New York Sun* gave it quite a story. I still have a clipping of the story.

'The man who runs the smallest post office in the United States today met the man who runs the biggest post office in the United States... Latham of Marshall Pass. Colo., whose four-foot square post office is the smallest and Albert Goldman, whose modest establishment . . . New York, is the biggest, found that about the only thing that their offices had

*Gustavus A. Latham, U.S. Postmaster at Marshall Pass 1930 to 1952.*
Dow Helmers Collection

*in common were scratchy pens. Marshall Pass is a railroad station on the Continental Divide, over 10,000 feet above sea level, Latham said, and the total population is eleven persons, plus a couple of itinerant mountain lions and a hound dog or two.*

*'The post office occupies a corner of the railroad depot and consists of one table, one chair, four lock boxes, one post master and a few sundries such as $50.00 worth of stamps, envelopes and cards, Latham said.*

*'Latham struggles under the burden of six to nine incoming and outgoing letters a week. The post office does $1,200.00 business a year as compared with New York City's $143 million.*

*'Some postmasters may shovel snow in their spare time and give full time to the mail, but Latham shovels snow as a full time job and gives his spare time to the mail. This is because there is more snow than mail at Marshall Pass. He earns $1,600 a year doing away with snowpiles for the Denver & Rio Grande Railroad and $201 a year doing away with mailpiles for Uncle Sam.'*

Paul Phelan, *New York Sun,* October 19, 1948

"After I got home from the New York convention, I got 1,238 letters from all over the world.
"I believe Marshall Pass has recorded wrecks every year since it was built. One of the Parlin

*Engine 483 slowly rolls past the Sargent depot as it prepares to take water prior to its departure, eastbound for Marshall Pass.*　　　　　　　　　　　　　　　　　　　　　　　　JACKSON C. THODE PHOTO, DOW HELMERS COLLECTION

boys was killed on a runaway engine. Engineer Shaw was crippled for life. The worst runaway in my time was at Mears Junction. The engineer and fireman jumped off, but seven men were killed.

"In that day we had a quarter of a mile of sheds and a turntable. There were eight freight trains a day and two passenger trains, one each way. There was thirteen months that I never came to town. I let my whiskers grow and stayed right there.

"Soon after the railroad was built to Shirley, Bonanza built a tram line over the top of the mountain to bring the ore, in buckets, to be loaded on the cars at Shirley. It was much faster and cheaper to tram the ore over the mountain than freight it from Bonanza to Villa Grove.

"No, there were no accommodations at Marshall Pass for tourists, but countless people came up on the morning train which arrived at 9:00 A.M., bringing their lunches with them, to climb Mount Ouray or hike along the crest of the divide to where they could look down on Bonanza. A few would ride up on the cars and hike back to Mears Junction via the old (Mears) wagon road. Those up top would board the eastbound train at 7:25 P.M. It made a wonderful day. I myself climbed to the top of Mount Ouray the first day I was there. It was on the Fourth of July and the climb took me four hours.

"The station on Marshall burned down in 1923. The [snow] shed, too, caught afire, but they cut it in two and saved about 300 feet of it. The depot was so badly damaged that they tore the brick building down and built a new one out of frame.

'There was one good mine on Marshall Pass. They shipped forty-three cars of fluorspar from it while I was there. The loading ramp is there yet, just above my houses. Both of those buildings on the pass belong to me. They were originally built for the section men. After I retired I bought the buildings up there. I also own the old depot at Poncha. I have spent many, many of my summers living in one of these houses on the Pass. In fact, I plan to go up there again this summer.

"In 1952 the railroad moved the men down to Poncha Springs and we stayed there a year. They then told us to go to Salida. I rode the last train, in 1954, to Crested Butte. I was in Poncha at the time and was called to get on this train. Going up, just exactly a mile this side at Parlin curve (Parlin tank) the snow was deep. They rammed the two engines and two cabooses and the snowplow into it and then couldn't back out. All the men got out and I walked over the top of the train and when I went over the engine, I stepped into the smoke stack and one leg went clear down.

"One day while I was struggling with the heavy slag and those nine-foot creosoted ties, I remembered that I was sixty-nine years old and I said to myself, 'If I have to wear a pick out from 8 o'clock until 10 o'clock and then wear another out from 10 o'clock until 12 o'clock, then man-handle those ties all afternoon, well, why not go fishin'?' . . . I retired!"

## Bill Ausmus
### Sargent, Colorado

*Bill Ausmus was twenty-four in 1908 when he went to work for the Rio Grande Railroad. He worked out of Salida and, after due time was promoted from fireman to engineer. He has lived most of his 83 years in and around Sargent, Colorado, where I visited with him on a bright, crisp day in February, 1967 and asked questions about his experiences on the old narrow gauge over Marshall Pass.*

"You must remember it has been many, many years since I worked over Marshall. Oh, sure, I had lots of experiences—every railroader who worked over that hill had experiences. Yes, there are a couple that come to mind, now that you ask," he said, as he settled back in his chair and looked distrustfully at my tape recorder, which was quickly forgotten as old memories came rushing back.

*Mount Ouray keeps a commanding watch over the Marshall Pass route as #490 moves up grade above Shirley with a long string of empty stock cars bound for the Gunnison Valley. Stock traffic was a chief source of revenue during the last years of the route's operation.*   COLORADO HISTORICAL SOCIETY

*Patterns of sunlight, coming through the breaks in the snowshed roof, create a dramatic effect as the trainmen converse during the Marshall Pass stop. First car on engine 470's drawbar is an RPO car.*
PHOTO BY G. M. BEST, DOW HELMERS COLLECTION

"One night on the pass, shortly after I had gone to work for the railroad, I was firing No. 229 when she dropped her crown sheet. We had pulled to a stop, going up, just above Grays to take water. I had just got down and put in fire.

"You know, those 200s were deckless engines. They had a cab door on the engineer's side and a cab door on the fireman's side. I had just gotten back into my cab, alongside the boilerhead and was looking out the window at the snow, when it happened. I sailed out that window like a bird! The engineer never got off at all, he sat right on the engine. The explosion had blown the coal gates out and swept that tank so clean that, if I had been down there putting in fire, I would never had known what hit me!

"Another time, we were coming downgrade with four empty "gons" and a coach. This was with No. 229, too. I was firing for an engineer named Dawson, who had not been on the road very long and wasn't familiar with the hill. I knew the physical characteristics of the grade pretty well. We had passed over a stretch that was nearly level, and when we reached a tip-over and headed down a more severe grade, Dawson made a reduction in his train line, five or six pounds. He watched closely for a little while and when he saw it didn't do much good, he made another reduction. Then he turned around and looked at me and said, 'Is this train holding all right?'

*No. 483, with fresh snow on its plow, pauses on the Chester siding to allow a string of empties to pass en route to the summit.* ROBERT W. RICHARDSON PHOTO, DOW HELMERS COLLECTION

"I told him that it wasn't and that we were starting to run away. Then I shouted to him to give her everything he had and to whistle for brakes. He did this, but our train kept going and kept gaining speed.

"When Dawson asked what to do next, I advised him to reverse his engine, open the cylinder cocks and put on the driving brakes. Our drag was going so fast by this time, that Dawson was too frightened to think clearly. Roy Sloane was conductor of the train and he had been trying to pull the slack up with the coach, so he could cut off this car with the passengers.

"When Dawson reversed the engine and set his driving brakes, that put a hump against the train and let the conductor cut the coach loose. The two brakemen were up on top setting hand brakes and the fire was flying out of the wheels, clear out to the sides.

"We were coming down that hill real fast, now so when the engineer asked me again what we should do, I simply replied that we had done everything humanly possible to stop that train but nothing had worked, so it was every fellow for himself. I had just seen the two brakemen jump, and I told Dawson I was going to jump. I knew we were coming to a spot on the north side of the track that was sort of like a little park and did not have very many rocks. I climbed down on the step and when we got to this place I let go and rolled clear across the clearing and hit my nose on a big rock on the other side.

*Long stock extra slowly approaches the top of Marshall Pass, eastbound.*
ROBERT W. RICHARDSON PHOTO, DOW HELMERS COLLECTION

*Sixteen car stock extra, powered by three powerful little narrow gauge locomotives, passes Tank Seven.*
ROBERT W. RICHARDSON PHOTO, DOW HELMERS COLLECTION

"It didn't knock me out but it sure gave me a good jolt and dazed me for a spell. Dawson was still on the engine. He was a heavy set fellow and not too active. The train went around a turn and entered a cut and Dawson jumped just as it came out of that cut.

"By the time I got up, the train had gone by me. I started walking down the track. Dawson had jumped on the uphill side and came up the track to meet me.

"He said, 'My goodness, aren't you killed? I thought every bone in your body was broken when I seen you hit the ground.' I replied, 'I don't believe I'm hurt as bad as you are.' 'Oh,' he said, 'I'm not hurt.' I asked, 'What is that running down your forehead?' He put his hands up there and it nearly scared him to death, when he saw them covered with blood.

"About that time the conductor came along down with the coach and picked us up. Our train had gone on until it hit a curve and a cut. The engine had gone in the ditch and the four gons had stacked right up on each other and on the engine. Darndest thing you ever saw! We looked the wreckage over but there was nothing we could do, so we climbed back to the grade and walked on down the hill with Sloane and his seven or eight passengers. Finally we got a push car and got orders from the dispatcher at Salida. We went to Salida, all of us, on the handcar. It was all down-grade, you see.

"Dawson went to the hospital in Denver and died, soon after. After about three or four days, I signed a release and went back to work. You can see, here, that I got a good jolt on my nose, it has never been straight since then.

"Sargents was a helper station at that time. There was a big wye over beyond the depot, and I have seen as many as eighteen or twenty locomotives in this yard. Bill Cole was agent here at Sargents and for a long spell they had three operators—it was a busy town. One of the little 200s that I worked on is the 268 now in the museum over at Gunnison."

Bill Ausmus' picturesque, comfortable little home, is located facing the old Rio Grande mainline, as it entered Sargent, and it was with a tear in his eye that Bill wistfully said, "Even now in the deep of the night I still hear those wonderful little trains, whistling their way into the yards here at Sargents."

*"Stock extra east" September 1953, saw this dramatic scene as four husky steam locomotives head east from Sargent to Marshall Pass with full tonnage. Stock train was loaded at Parlin.*
JOHNNY KRAUSE PHOTO, DOW HELMERS COLLECTION

# VI

# Tunnels, Highways, and Fading Whistles

*Engine 480, with caboose 0589 on its drawbar, has just turned off from the Marshall Pass mainline and will turn onto the crossover trestle. The string of coal-loaded gondolas is on track No. 12, a spur. Engine 482, in the foreground, is headed for the San Luis Valley via Poncha Pass, taking the final train to be scheduled from Salida to Alamosa, February 14, 1951.*
Robert W. Richardson photo, Dow Helmers Collection

# VI | Tunnels, Highways, and Fading Whistles

*We find that the present and future public convenience and necessity permit abandonment by the Denver & Rio Grande Western Railroad Company of the lines of railroad in Chaffee, Saguache and Gunnison Counties, Colorado, described herein.*

INTERSTATE COMMERCE COMMISSION Div. 4
December A.D. 1953
George W. Laird, Secretary

As the aspens turned to gold in the fall of 1912, the idea of broad-gauging the Marshall Pass line became little more than talk, and the once-proud main line of Palmer's Rio Grande empire settled into the role of a country railroad. Tourists still rode the train during the summer to stare at the scenery and late summer and early fall found the Rio Grande busy handling a variety of ranching and agricultural products on their way to the markets of the Eastern Slope. Yet, gone was the bustle of transcontinental traffic. The slowness of trains was almost as traditional in the United States as apple pie, and in these waning years the line over Marshall Pass was no exception. Gunnisonites were fond of saying that the Rio Grande was "on time any time," and Gunnison old-timers philosophically declared that "the reason you didn't want the Rio Grande to run over you was because it was on you so long." Still, there was a close identification between the narrow gauge and the communities it served; and, while in 1912, that identification had begun to fade, it would be more than four decades before black smoke and steam no longer pierced the skies over Marshall Pass.

After 1912, there was no denying that the broad gauging ideas had become little more than talk, but there was something about that kind of talk that kept a spark of hope in Gunnison businessmen and Chamber of Commerce supporters. Time and time again after 1912, articles appeared in Gunnison papers asserting that broad-gauging was on the way. A year after his initial comments, Rio Grande President Benjamin F. Bush again assured the state that broad-gauging Marshall Pass was still foremost in Rio Grande plans. The 135 miles between Salida and Montrose were to be broad-gauged at the cost of $3,000,000, one million more than the 1912 estimate, as part of extensive improvements along the entire system. "The estimates have been completed for broad-gauging this line and just as soon as the money market improves, we expect to start work," said President Bush.[1] The perpetual problem was that the money market never seemed to improve, and whatever boom the broad gauge might have been to the Western Slope economy, there was no way of forcing the building of the line.

In the summer of 1914, during one of the Rio Grande's periodic financial upheavals, famed engineer John F. Stevens was hired by bankers who held Rio Grande paper, to make an inspection of the system. The inspection was to ascertain the line's current condition and its expected earning power. The only narrow gauge segment which Stevens found in acceptable condition was the line over Marshall Pass between Salida and Montrose.[2] While this in itself was a plus for Marshall Pass, it should be noted that aside from the Antonito-Durango-Silverton run, Marshall Pass was the only large narrow gauge route left in the system.

VI | TUNNELS, HIGHWAYS, AND FADING WHISTLES | 119

*On the rear of this passenger train, westbound for Marshall Pass, is a jaunty little narrow gauge observation car, sporting a drumhead which identifies the train as the "Shawano." It has just pulled away from Mears Junction and is passing the switch for the Villa Grove branch which crosses the trestle at right and climbs along the side of the opposite hill. The Marshall Pass mainline goes under the trestle and up the valley at right; August 1, 1938.*
RICHARD B. JACKSON PHOTO, DOW HELMERS COLLECTION

*Westbound train No. 315, the "Shawano" with three head-end revenue cars, including the "Salida & Montrose" RPO car and two coaches, nearing the station of Otto, 8.7 miles west of Salida, on August 14, 1939.*
RICHARD B. JACKSON PHOTO, DOW HELMERS COLLECTION

Events elsewhere during the summer of 1914 set the world aflame. However, World War I was slow to be felt by the Rio Grande, and it was 1917 before the Marshall Pass line was busy moving products for a war-time economy. Cattle, coal, fruit, and agricultural products were hauled eastward across the pass to support the boys who had gone "over there." When the war ended, attention shifted back to the home front and once more thought was given to broad-gauging Marshall Pass. In January of 1919, the Colorado Senate passed a resolution requesting that broad-gauging of Marshall Pass be undertaken at once. As usual, the resolution contained glowing phrases boasting of the great value of such a project to the economy of the Western Slope. In addition, Congressman Edward Taylor was reported to be applying pressure in Washington for federal assistance for the project.[3] A month later, Gunnison's Chamber of Commerce announced that one of its major goals for 1919 would be to see that the switch to standard gauge was made over Marshall Pass.[4] The movement seemed to be on its way.

Then, in April, news from Denver gave a new twist to the broad gauge battle. Western Slope senators and representatives attempted to attach an amendment to the Moffat Tunnel Bill calling for a similar tunnel under Marshall Pass. The Moffat Tunnel under James Peak was proposed to give Denver a direct railroad connection west to Salt Lake City and eliminate treacherous Rollins Pass. Western Slope lawmakers saw hope that a similar project could be initiated for Marshall Pass. Such a project was sure to bring about broad-gauging and would greatly benefit

*"The engine bell will toll the death knell." Train No. 315, the "Shawano" powered by engine 479 on the final westbound passenger run, through a fairyland of beauty, on November 24, 1940. "The narrow ribbons of steel over which it rolled has become a sanctified trail." (Quotes from Frank E. Gimlett)*

JACKSON C. THODE PHOTO, DOW HELMERS COLLECTION

*Engine No. 479 dutifully takes the four cars of "The Shawano" across the main range on its final run, November 24, 1940.*
JACKSON C. THODE PHOTO, DOW HELMERS COLLECTION

the development of the Western Slope. The Senate approved the amendment, but the House defeated the measure 33-31.[5] Still, the idea to tunnel under Marshall Pass was revived.

Along with the Moffat Tunnel proposal came plans for the Dotsero Cutoff, a thirty-eight mile section linking the Denver and Salt Lake Railroad with the Rio Grande line west from Tennessee Pass to Grand Junction. Such a cutoff would give Denver the long-desired direct line to Salt Lake City. The *Gunnison News-Champion* of April 25 carried a letter by State Senator George Hetherington stating that if the Moffat Tunnel and the Dotsero Cutoff were approved, the only way for southwestern Colorado to retain its share of commerce and transportation would be to tunnel under Marshall Pass and broad-gauge the line from Salida to Montrose.[6]

On April 24, a Denver conference concerning the proposed tunnels was held with approximately twenty-five delegates in attendance. Carrol M. Carter and H. C. Bartlett, Gunnison's Chamber of Commerce representatives, reported that all of the delegates showed intense interest in the Moffat Tunnel, but also were in favor of including the Marshall Pass Tunnel to insure the former's construction. Carter and Bartlett concluded that Denver interests would eventually build the Moffat Tunnel and Dotsero Cutoff regardless. Consequently, it was necessary to include Marshall Pass in the initial plans or southwestern Colorado would be left with a narrow gauge line indefinitely.[7]

Throughout the controversy many people used the locations of Monarch Pass and Marshall Pass interchangeably. Everyone wanted a tunnel through the Continental Divide in that general

*Often called the "Salida-Montrose" train by local people, the picturesque narrow gauge consist moves gracefully into the viewfinder of Richard B. Jackson's camera, near Otto, on July 8, 1940.*
RICHARD B. JACKSON PHOTO, DOW HELMERS COLLECTION

*"As I look through the windows of that little train for the last time ... the empty seats will seem but crypts." - Frank E. Gimlett. Train No. 316, eastbound, ready to depart Gunnison on its final run over Marshall Pass, November 24, 1940.*
JACKSON C. THODE PHOTO, DOW HELMERS COLLECTION

vicinity, but they were divided on whether to build under Marshall Pass or Monarch Pass. A. E. Reynolds, aging mining tycoon of the San Juans, wrote the Colorado Railroad Commission in October of 1919, urging tunnel construction in southwestern Colorado. Reynolds, however, urged that not a dollar be spent on broad-gauging Marshall Pass, but rather, that a tunnel be built under Monarch Pass, and then that the entire section be broad-gauged.[8] Regardless of whether one favored Monarch Pass or Marshall Pass, support continued to come from all corners urging construction of a tunnel.

One of the most far-sighted pleas for tunnel construction came from Charles A. Lory, President of the State Agricultural College at Fort Collins, in a letter to William G. Evans, President of the Colorado Railroad Commission. In the letter, Lory urged the construction of tunnels under James Peak and Marshall Pass. The Moffat Tunnel under James Peak would lead to the Dotsero Cutoff and eliminate the circuitous southern route through Pueblo required to get from Denver to Grand Junction. To appease the people of Pueblo and the Arkansas Valley, who might be upset at the loss of trade on the Royal Gorge route, the Marshall Pass Tunnel and new broad gauge would bring increased transcontinental and state traffic along the southern route. Summing up his argument, Lory proclaimed, "Colorado must set itself the task of opening this great region to further development. A double-tracked tunnel thru James Peak, the Dotsero Cutoff, a broad gauge from Montrose to Salida, and a broad gauge from Del Norte to Durango will form the best possible investment."[9] Lory's observations were practical and had the support of many, but as supporters of Marshall Pass were to learn, popular support did not always lead to positive action.

In late December, the Railroad Commission recommended to Governor Oliver Shoup that tunnels be built under James Peak, Marshall Pass, and Cumbres Pass on the Antonito to

*No. 315, the "Shawano" makes an appealing picture as it slips smoothly across the truss bridge over the Arkansas River, westbound for Marshall Pass behind engine No. 479. In the background is Tenderfoot Mountain.*
RICHARD B. JACKSON PHOTO, DOW HELMERS COLLECTION

*August 14, 1939 found Richard B. Jackson waiting to board the westbound "Shawano" at Salida. The little narrow gauge passenger train is being switched by standard gauge engine 1173, while the famous Monte Cristo Hotel looks on.*
RICHARD B. JACKSON PHOTO, DOW HELMERS COLLECTION

Durango run. Detailed cost estimates of the projects were not available; however, the Commission was sure that the cost would be justified in terms of long range investment.[10] A week later, Horace Wilcox, editor of the *Rocky Mountain News*, in the 1920 New Year's edition of the paper called for a six-mile tunnel under Monarch Pass, a six and four-tenths-mile tunnel under James Peak, and a shorter tunnel under Cumbres Pass.[11] Again, there was support for the tunnels, although the debate between Monarch Pass and Marshall Pass continued.

In early March of 1920 the *News-Champion* ran a banner headline proclaiming "Three Tunnel Project Wins United Support of Colorado." On March 1, 1920, at a meeting of mayors and town representatives in Denver's City Auditorium, the Railroad Commission unveiled the three tunnel or tri-tunnel project, as it came to be called. The proposal for tunnels under James Peak, Marshall Pass, and Cumbres Pass was given almost unanimous support. The only region opposed to the proposal was southeastern Colorado where people refused to give up their monopoly on Denver to Salt Lake City traffic through the Royal Gorge. Two points were made at the conference which were important to the Western Slope. First was the definite need for a tunnel under either Marshall Pass or Monarch Pass if the section between Salida and Montrose was ever to be broad-gauged. Second was the consensus of Western Slope representatives that the bill for the tunnels should provide for simultaneous construction. This would eliminate the possibility of the Moffat Tunnel being constructed first and the remaining projects then halted by Denver politicians.[12]

Because the three tunnels. in the proposal were to be owned and operated by the State of Colorado at an estimated initial expense of $18,500,000, the issue had to be approved by the voters of the state. Fiery orators traveled the state speaking in support of the plan. Even the weather contributed a supporting hand by disrupting travel on the passes with an exceptionally vicious

*Salida from Tenderfoot Hill with the Marshall Pass right of way clearly visible crossing the trestle at lower left and stretching west toward Mount Ouray.*
DOW HELMERS COLLECTION

*"End of 3rd Rail" is now "End of the Iron Trail." Narrow gauge rails of the Rio Grande point bravely at the snow caps of the Continental Divide, as they aim for Marshall Pass.*
NEAL R. MILLER PHOTO, DOW HELMERS COLLECTION

*On a beautiful winter day, in February, 1951, engine 480 with caboose 0589, moves slowly across the trestle over the Marshall Pass mainline at Mears Junction.*

ROBERT W. RICHARDSON PHOTO, DOW HELMERS COLLECTION

*Engine 492 powers a short consist of gondolas toward the cross-over of the Marshall Pass mainline, en route to the San Luis Valley via Poncha Pass and Villa Grove.*

ROBERT W. RICHARDSON PHOTO, DOW HELMERS COLLECTION

spring snowstorm; this was followed by flooding along the Arkansas River which disrupted traffic on the Royal Gorge route. Both these occurrences were ammunition for the advocates of the tunnels. But the oratory and weather were not enough. On November 2, 1920, when the nation was rallying to Warren G. Harding, the voters of Colorado rejected the tri-tunnel amendment by 10,000 votes. Denver carried the measure by almost three to one, but Pueblo and southeastern Colorado, out to hold on to the Royal Gorge route monopoly, soundly rejected the plan.[13]

The setback disheartened many of those who had led the fight for the tunnels, particularly the big tunnel west of Denver. But the hard core enthusiasts, like William Evans of the Railroad Commission, showed no indication of giving up. If the state did not want the tri-tunnel project, that was its own doing; Denver would have its tunnel regardless! The fear that Western Slope residents had voiced over the previous year came true, and once the tunnel west of Denver was constructed and the Dotsero Cutoff completed, there was little hope of additional construction on the Marshall Pass and Durango lines.

While the Denver group went on with the fight for the Moffat Tunnel, Gunnisonites came up with another plan which only served to divide the supporters of a Monarch-Marshall Tunnel further. The plan presented by the *News Champion* called for a tunnel to be built under Altman Pass. It was to be lower and much longer than the Alpine Tunnel, which the Denver, South Park, and Pacific had finally abandoned in 1910. The paper proposed that the Rio Grande could use much of the South Park roadbed and that a lower tunnel of at least six miles in length would

*Long drag of box cars, eastbound, up from Sargent, pauses before entering the snowsheds on the west side of Marshall Pass. The headend helper engine has been cut off and has entered the snowsheds where it will turn on the turntable.*
ROBERT W. RICHARDSON PHOTO, DOW HELMERS COLLECTION

*Engine 479 about to enter the Marshall Pass snowsheds, pulling the "Shawano" westbound from Salida to Gunnison, July 30, 1938.*  RICHARD B. JACKSON PHOTO, DOW HELMERS COLLECTION

eliminate much of the snow removal problems which had plagued the South Park. In an interesting footnote, the *News-Champion* related that the reason the South Park had so much trouble with the Alpine Tunnel was because the Rio Grande had bribed the South Park engineer to place the east portal of the tunnel on a north-facing slope. This meant that the ice and snow would be melted out only in the summer months.[14] Certainly there is little credibility to the story, particularly when one notes that the position of the tunnel on a portion of the Divide which runs almost east to west leaves little choice but to have the east portal on a north-facing slope. At any rate, it gave the move for a new Alpine Tunnel one more shot-in-the-arm, and left Marshall Pass even farther away from getting a tunnel.

While dissension caused a drop in interest in a tunnel through the Divide in the Marshall Pass region, Denver supporters of the Rio Grande got behind the Moffat Tunnel effort and completed the bore under James Peak by 1927. Seven years later on June 16, 1934, the Dotsero Cutoff was formally opened and the Denver and Salt Lake Railroad west from Denver joined with the main line of the Rio Grande to Grand Junction to give Denver at long last a direct railroad connection west to Salt Lake City. Arkansas Valley residents, who might have enjoyed a broad gauge line over Marshall Pass if they had not been so greedy for a monopoly of the Royal Gorge route in 1920, now were placed on the secondary route through Colorado. Marshall Pass and the residents of the Western Slope were even more adversely affected as there was now nothing short of a miracle that could bring about a broad gauge road. The fears voiced by Chamber of Commerce representatives Bartlett and Carter at the 1919 convention had come true. Denver had built the Moffat Tunnel and Dotsero Cutoff without regard to the actions of the rest of the state. Because the Marshall Pass area could not begin to equal the political and financial clout of Denver, the region could not take the same "we'll build regardless" attitude. Thus, southwestern Colorado was left to the narrow gauge indefinitely, and the Marshall Pass line settled deeper into its role of a sleepy country railroad.

Still, there was excitement on the pass. Who could forget the Fourth of July on Marshall Pass when the snowsheds and depot burned? It was 1923 and sparks either from a carelessly thrown firecracker or a passing engine ignited the blaze which burned two hundred feet of the snowsheds on the summit's east side. The depot and some surrounding buildings were also engulfed. Fifty men were put to work clearing the track and laying 1,000 feet of new rail to replace that warped by the blaze. By 11:30 the next morning traffic was again rolling on the line. The Rio Grande was congratulated on its quick work by the *News Champion*, which noted that the mail would not be late.[15]

Yet, times were changing. With the 1920s a new level of prosperity was achieved, and with it were signs that things would never be quite the same again. Dapper young gentlemen now spent Sunday afternoons courting the ladies of their fancy in automobiles. Those not so fortunate were hopeful that their ladies would not think them bores if they rode the afternoon excursion to the top of Marshall Pass, a ride which would have thrilled their mothers. Yes, times were changing. For Marshall Pass, the 1920s was a decade of quiet transition. The pass and railroad had disappeared from the headlines and settled into the role of a quietly reliable and slowly fading servant. No construction was undertaken, the horrible train wrecks had virtually disappeared as less traffic moved, and the tunnel and broad-gauging project had become only a memory. So the pass and the railroad faithfully acted out their roles waiting until controversy over highways and abandonments brought their names back into the head lines once again.

While the "Roaring Twenties" were not as roaring on Marshall Pass as elsewhere, Prohibition was bound to have an influence on the pass, just as it did on the rest of the nation. Early

*"The town, the tracks and the train." This was Sargent, Colorado, on August 29, 1935, photographed from the coal chute, looking west. On the main line, standing in front of the depot (hidden by the water tank) is the Gunnison bound passenger train. Track 39 passes in front of sand houses and curves to the right, being one leg of the wye. Three strings of gondolas, set out to wait for the turn-around crews to take them up the hill, are heaped high with Crested Butte coal.*
RICHARD B. JACKSON PHOTO, DOW HELMERS COLLECTION

*Aerial view of Marshall Pass, approaching the summit eastbound, flying above Marshall Creek at the approximate confluence of Tank Seven Creek.*
DOW HELMERS COLLECTION

*While road engine 483 takes water at Shawano, helper engine 489 awaits its turn at the end of an eastbound stock train. Mount Ouray in background.*
JACKSON C. THODE PHOTO, DOW HELMERS COLLECTION

one morning, an old-timer started up the pass from Sargent with a wagon containing several kegs of a highly controversial liquid. In good Snuffy Smith fashion, the sheriff and revenuers were informed of his cargo and set up a trap at the top of the pass. Whether the old-timer was informed of the trap or whether he dropped his cargo before reaching the summit according to plan is not known; however, upon searching his wagon at the summit, the revenuers found nothing incriminating. Just where those kegs went remains a mystery. Some say, however, that in the days immediately following, the engines taking on water at Tank Seven seemed to chug up the pass with just a little more steam and drive than usual, as if something more potent than water was boiling inside.

Not all incidents on Marshall Pass in the 1930s had quite the tongue-in-cheek flavor of the preceding decade. In February of 1938, three Gunnison businessmen, Wes McDermott, Charles Sweitzer, and Rial Lake, organized a special excursion train to the top of the pass to publicize the skiing potential of the Gunnison country. A special made up of four coaches, a combination baggage and coach, and a baggage car left Gunnison at 8:45 on Sunday morning, February 13, with 137 Gunnison, Montrose, and Baldwin ski buffs for the summit of the pass. After reaching the summit about 11:00 A.M., the group spent the next five hours skiing and tobogganing between the summit and Shawano, a vertical drop of seven hundred feet. The train was initially scheduled to make a run every forty-five minutes to haul the skiers back to the summit from Shawano. Actually, only three runs were made, yet every one seemed to get in plenty of skiing under a clear and sunny sky, which lacked one of Marshall Pass's closest companions—wind.

A group of Salida promoters had organized a similar venture from their side of the Divide and their arrival made for quite a lively and crowded afternoon. Such personalities as Count

*Looking south down the summit siding to the west end of the summit snowsheds; mainline is below right.*
ROBERT W. RICHARDSON PHOTO, DOW HELMERS COLLECTION

Phillipe de Pret, Belgian professional skier, T. J. Flynn, owner of the Aspen ski course, Thomas Groswald, well-known manufacturer of skis, and Frank Ashley, champion ski jumper of the West, were all on hand to give instruction to those who requested it and laugh at those who should have. Despite a course that was soon littered with sitz marks and fallen skiers, only one serious injury occurred when Ruth Darby of Salida fell and broke her right leg.[16] Three Gunnisonites missed the returning train and had to ride back to town on one of the helper engines. They arrived safely, but were covered with soot from the dirt and smoke of the engine. Despite the publicity, the venture was not successful financially, and the three Gunnison promoters had to cough up fifty dollars of their own money to pay the railroad its charter fee.[17] The venture had, however, pointed the direction toward the winter potential of the Gunnison country as a recreational playground, although, somewhat sadly, the railroad would not be around to enjoy it.

The 1930s also saw the climax of the Marshall Pass–Monarch Pass controversy. As early as 1880, the rivalry of a toll road across Monarch Pass had prompted Otto Mears to sell his Marshall Pass Toll Road to the Rio Grande. Marshall Pass, largely because of Mears road, won the battle for the railroad. By the time the automobile came on the scene, Monarch Pass was back in the rivalry desperately lobbying for a road to be built across its slopes. By the fall of 1913, an auto road, though quite steep in places and with numerous switchbacks, was completed over the pass. Then in 1921, an improvement project on the road was completed, which reduced the grade to less than six per cent and lowered the crossing by one hundred and fifty feet.[18]

As U. S. Highway 50 was improved across the state, residents along the route in central Colorado began to clamor for a better crossing of the Continental Divide. One such promoter was W. H. Nelson, a life-long resident of Colorado, then residing in Norwood. In 1877, while in the cattle business, Nelson and his partner, George Nathrop, cut the first significant trail over Marshall Pass. During the following year, they worked for Otto Mears as he perfected the trail into his toll road. After serving in the state legislature and later as a county commissioner, Nelson wrote to Governor Ed Johnson in August of 1935 with regard to the need for an improved

*D&RGW 489, and six-car Rocky Mountain Railroad Club special at Poncha Pass May 21, 1950.*
JACKSON THODE PHOTO, DOW HELMERS COLLECTION

*Rocky Mountain Railroad Club excursion train creeps upgrade under the shadow of Mount Ouray on Marshall Pass in 1949.*   NEAL R. MILLER PHOTO, DOW HELMERS COLLECTION

crossing of the Divide. In doing so, he argued for changing the route from Monarch Pass to Marshall Pass. Nelson, though now past eighty, wrote of the gentle grade, the lower altitude, and the sunny southern slope of the pass he had worked on almost sixty years before.[19]

Nelson's letter along with many others prompted Governor Johnson to order Homer Gray, resident engineer at Gunnison, to conduct a preliminary survey in the fall of 1935 across Marshall Pass. Gray's reports were favorable and in May of 1936 the highway board voted its approval of Marshall Pass as the new route for Highway 50.[20] The board's resolution did not call for immediate action, nor did it provide for any specific plans. Consequently, no action was taken to begin surveying the new route. This delay greatly irked the citizens of Gunnison and other Western Slope communities who were anxious to have the survey completed in time for the road to become a part of the 1937 road budget. The Gunnison Chamber of Commerce sent a letter to Governor Johnson in mid-June which vigorously protested the lack of a survey and urged him to command State Highway Engineer Charles Vail to begin the survey immediately.[21] More letters of protest on the delay and petitions expounding on the virtues of Marshall Pass were sent to the Governor before he finally took action in mid-July and ordered Vail to make a detailed survey at once. Vail appointed R. E. Cowden, head locating engineer in the department, to make the survey.[22]

The survey was conducted and appropriations for the road over Marshall Pass were made a part of the 1937 state highway budget when it was drawn up in November of 1936. Approved by the highway advisory board and signed by Governor Johnson, the 1937 budget appropriated

*Looking northeast down the Marshall Pass mainline under the San Luis branch crossover to the Mears Junction tank.*
JACKSON THODE PHOTO, DOW HELMERS COLLECTION

$1,250,000 for the twenty-six miles of road between Mears Junction and Sargent. The battle for Marshall Pass seemed to be won and supporters along Highway 50 cheered. However, even in reporting the budget approval, the *Gunnison News-Champion* questioned whether this assured the pass construction. The paper noted that there was a difference of opinion on the status of the budget. Most authorities agreed that the signed budget was a legal document binding on the state for the next year, but a few people said that certain high officials in the road department could side-step the appropriation. In this particular case, "certain high officials" meant State Engineer Charles Vail.

Early in December, Vail met with Governor Johnson, who had been elected to the United States Senate during the fall election, and the leaders of the Highway 50 Association from Fremont, Chaffee, Gunnison, Montrose, and Delta Counties. Despite the urgings of the Association leaders, Vail voiced his opposition to the Marshall Pass appropriation. Even with Vail's objections, which at this time were somewhat vague, most people along the route were of the belief that the new governor, Teller Ammons, could not turn his back on Marshall Pass and would command Vail to undertake the project whether he liked it or not.[23]

A few days before the end of the year, Vail made headlines all along Highway 50 by refusing to sign the road budget because of the appropriation for Marshall Pass. By now he was able to give a clearer reason for his views, holding that the $1,250,000 designated for Marshall Pass should be used on Floyd Hill west of Denver instead. Vail's actions precipitated a major legal battle in which the state attorney general finally advised that it was not necessary for Vail to sign the budget for it to become effective and that once the budget was written, the state engineer could not substantially alter it.[24] Again it seemed that Vail had no choice but to build over Marshall Pass. For those who drew a parallel between this controversy and the "assurance" of a tunnel and broad gauge however, the outcome was still in doubt.

Nevertheless, the battle shaping up appeared very one sided; it involved the people of fifteen counties along Highway 50 versus Charles Vail. The *News-Champion* of January 28, 1937, ran a quick box score of the contest. First, there were the Marshall Pass supporters who had repeated the virtues of the pass at least a thousand times. Second, there was Charles Vail who contended that the benefits of Marshall Pass were not equal to the expense involved, and that once completed, its speed and safety would offer little more than could be obtained by spending less money and improving Monarch Pass. He also questioned whether the Marshall Pass route could be constructed for the amount appropriated. Finally, there was the compromise

*The narrow gauge iron curves gracefully across the apex of Marshall Pass, 10,846 feet above sea level. For many years, rail traffic was so dense, a double line was needed under the snowsheds. 1949 was much more quiet.*
NEAL R. MILLER PHOTO, DOW HELMERS COLLECTION

*The 1950 Rocky Mountain Railroad Club special crosses the Marshall Pass mainline bound for Poncha Pass.*
Jackson Thode photo, Dow Helmers Collection

view of the State Planning Commission which suggested moving the route of Highway 50 south. The highway would cross the Sangre de Cristo Mountains at Hayden Pass and proceed through Saguache over Cochetopa Pass into the Gunnison country. In an exchange characteristic of the battle, Vail further contended that because of mining activities there had to be a road over Monarch Pass anyway and that for $250,000 to $300,000 he could get Monarch in shape to serve as the highway as well. Responding, Charles Adams, Montrose publisher and president of the Highway 50 Association said, "Bull!" He had come over Marshall Pass in a wagon as a youngster and he declared it was the oldest and best crossing of the Continental Divide. Besides, Adams reasoned, if the road was built over Marshall Pass, the first ten miles of it from Salida to Mears Junction could be combined with U.S. 285 into the San Luis Valley which would save time and money.[25]

A week later the *News-Champion* ran a story stating that Governor Teller Ammons was considering directing three million dollars of the 1937 road budget toward Denver roads. Ammons had been accused of being a "Denver Man" during the campaign, but despite this charge, residents along the route could not believe that the governor would yield to Vail and "deprive us of Marshall Pass."[26] In the face of this new challenge, citizens in every county along Highway 50 launched a campaign of community boosterism for Marshall Pass, the likes of which had not been seen since the days of the initial rush of the railroads. Ads were placed in Denver papers extolling the good qualities of Marshall Pass. Pictures appeared in papers showing snow on Monarch Pass in June. The supporters of Marshall Pass claimed that their route would have no such problems. Chambers of Commerce from Pueblo to Grand Junction supported the route in letters and proclamations. Old-timers, like W. H. Nelson, wrote letters to the editors telling of early experiences on the pass and urging the construction of the proposed road.

Then, on June 17, 1937, in a pure case of "the votes are in the city, the country be damned," the *News-Champion* in bold headlines reported that Vail, with Governor Ammons's subtle approval had stolen a million dollars from Marshall Pass. Vail announced that tentatively $750,000 of the original appropriation would be used on Monarch Pass and the remainder on Cochetopa Pass. To the citizens along the route, this was getting two secondary crossings instead of the one good crossing that had been promised.[27] Politics had dealt William Marshall's short cut a dirty blow. Work started on Monarch Pass in October of 1938. When it was opened to the public on November 19, 1939, local residents who made the trip to the top were shocked to see a sign reading Vail Pass.[28] Their attitude was something less than benevolent and the sign quickly disappeared. Vail had won the battle, but he would have to go elsewhere if he wanted immortality on a mountain pass.

The highway which had provided so much controversy between Marshall Pass and Monarch Pass also made its weight felt on the railroad. In a prologue of what was to come, the Colorado Public Utilities Commission ruled in favor of the Denver and Rio Grande on June 27, 1936, and ordered the abandonment of passenger service between Gunnison and Montrose. Gunnisonites were disgruntled and the *News-Champion* called for plans to protest the ruling which

*The turntable, under the snowsheds, at the top of Marshall Pass, in 1955. The turntable was powered by air from the locomotives.*  NEAL R. MILLER PHOTO, DOW HELMERS COLLECTION

*Engine 489 coming off the wye at Sargent, to pick up a drag of drop-end gondolas, loaded with rails, removed from the mainline west of Sargent.*   ROBERT W. RICHARDSON PHOTO, DOW HELMERS COLLECTION

they termed unjust.[29] Nothing came of the protest and when the Rio Grande filed a petition for the abandonment of passenger service between Salida and Gunnison over Marshall Pass on September 18, 1940, there was little doubt what the final outcome would be. Still, Gunnison residents were unwilling to give up the railroad without a fight. The local Chamber of Commerce appointed a special railroad committee to protest the abandonment and in the event of an adverse ruling to urge certain demands in the abandonment order. Primarily, these demands included adequate bus service both east to Denver and west to Grand Junction, and the adjustment of schedules of branch bus lines to coincide with the main service. Guarantees were also sought for new facilities and new equipment on the bus routes.[30]

Finally on November 4, 1940, the day before a hectic national election, the Public Utilities Commission issued the order for all passenger service between Gunnison and Salida to cease on November 20. In one concession to residents of the Gunnison country, the order included the provision that in case of bad weather or poor road conditions, rail service would be re-established on a temporary basis. That may have pleased some old-timers who were skeptical of bus service over Monarch Pass, but to those with any forward directions it was clear that passenger service over Marshall Pass was gone for good. In adjusting to the new developments, the *News Champion* went to great lengths to discuss the new bus and mail schedules.[31] Three weeks later on Sunday, November 24, 1940, the passenger train "Shawano" made its last regularly scheduled run out of Gunnison and disappeared forever over the Divide to the east.[32]

Six months after the "Shawano" made its last run, the famed correspondent, Ernie Pyle, rode over the pass in the caboose of a freight train and wrote a column about his experiences.

VI | TUNNELS, HIGHWAYS, AND FADING WHISTLES | 139

Pyle was particularly impressed by the skill of the mountain railroaders.

*The top of Marshall Pass is just a few feet under 11,000. You feel it in your breathing when you get that high. Up there at the top is a great long snowshed through which the tracks run, as through a tunnel.*

*Inside it is a small turn-table where the extra engines are turned around and sent back down to Salida. We had only one engine coming down the pass, and needed it only for the brakes. The throttle was never opened.*

*Engineer Frank Frantz was the one who brought us down. It was fascinating to watch him work the air-brake lever. He didn't always put it on ahead of a curve, where you'd think he would. He seemed to do it at odd moments without any plan or purpose.*

*But then I learned that what he was doing was an absolute art. He wasn't merely judging the track ahead. He was judging, out of his mind and experience, all the long train behind us, and all the unseen curves over which we in the engine had already passed. He was handling the whole train with almost the rhythm of a crawling snake.*

*Engineers in this part of the world all have to be good "air men." That's the term used to designate their ability to handle a train smoothly on mountain grades with the air brakes. They say the best "air men" in America are right here on this narrow-gauge Marshall Pass division of the Denver & Rio Grande. My old hat is off to them.*[33]

Pyle was also greatly impressed with the beauty of the route and asked why some tourist agency did not make up a small circle trip to take a carload of tourists over and back. Before any

As #489 left the summit snowsheds, Otto C. Perry captured this historic picture of the last cattle train to be taken east over Marshall Pass. The date is October 9, 1953, and the end of an era is at hand.

O. C. PERRY, DENVER PUBLIC LIBRARY - WESTERN HISTORY DEPARTMENT

*In the dim light of the summit snowshed, No. 489 appears as a ghostly reminder of the days when the summit hummed with activity. The rails have already been removed from the ties on the second track and it will be only a matter of days before the steam engine is gone from Marshall Pass.* PAUL BRINKERHOFF

enterprising promoters could take up the idea, Pyle was off to Europe to write of less pleasant topics and the Rio Grande was thrown into doing its share for the war effort. During the war years, with the shortage of trucks and gasoline, the line hauled a great volume of local freight as well as products that were destined for further shipment from Salida to all points of the country. When the war ended, trucks, which were faster, cheaper, and more versatile, soon began to take a huge chunk out of the Rio Grande's business.

With decreasing tonnage in freight, the only bright spot left on the Marshall Pass run was the occasional excursion run over the pass by regional railroad clubs. One such excursion was sponsored in September of 1948 by the Rocky Mountain Railroad Club. A double-header train pulling eleven cars loaded with three hundred railroad buffs left Salida at 8:00 A.M. Saturday, September 18, and spent the day winding over the pass to Gunnison. As in Ernest Ingersoll's day, a stop was made at the summit to allow the tourists a chance to look around and take photographs of a vanishing era. The tour spent Saturday night in Gunnison, with many of the excursionists staying in private homes because of a lack of hotel and motel space. Early Sunday morning the train was run west to Cimarron to give the group one of the last views of the Black Canyon from the railroad tracks. A mechanical failure in the engine caused a two hour delay at Sapinero on the return trip so the tour was late in getting back to Gunnison. At Sargent, two helper engines were hooked on for the climb over Marshall Pass. With the helpers, the excursion train "went up in style" at a speed of twenty-five miles an hour, arriving at Salida at 8:00 P.M. that evening.[34] Even though tours such as this were frequent in the waning years of the railroad's service over Marshall Pass, they could not begin to make up for the loss in passenger and freight revenues. By the beginning of the 1950s the question of abandonment of the line was no longer "will they?" but merely, "when?"

# VI | Tunnels, Highways, and Fading Whistles

The first abandonment came on September 30, 1952, when the Rio Grande closed the station on the summit of the pass. With its closing, one of the pass's more colorful institutions died. Shortly after the railroad was built, the Post Office Department established the Marshall Pass Post Office. Many tourists mailed cards and letters from the summit for the Marshall Pass postmark as a collector's item. But, this too was now only a memory from the past, and when the station closed in September of 1952, Postmaster Gus Latham gathered up his supplies and money and put out the "closed" sign for the last time.

The following May a hearing was held in Salida before Paul C. Albus of the Interstate Commerce Commission to consider a motion by the Denver and Rio Grande Western Railroad to abandon the narrow gauge segment between Salida and Gunnison. At the hearing, T. K. Moriarty of the Rio Grande presented a list of thirty-six items demonstrating that maintaining the route was financially unfeasible. Opposition leaders, primarily mining concerns at Crested Butte and a lumber mill at Sapinero, contended that the railroad had made no effort to attract business and in some cases even discouraged it. When asked if the present high price of salvage had anything to do with the abandonment, Moriarty emphatically answered no, and said that operating losses were the only consideration in abandoning the route.[35] Despite vigorous arguments put forth by businessmen of the Gunnison country, Rio Grande operating losses could not be denied. The route had lost $146,338 in 1950, $205,781 in 1951, and $175,141 in 1952. In 1953, between the first of the year and the date of the hearing, the Rio Grande operated only four trains carrying revenue freight over the Marshall Pass line.[36] With the facts put forth, there was little mystery at what the final ruling of the Interstate Commerce Commission would be.

*#489 drifts downgrade out of the eastern end of the summit snowsheds.*
ROBERT W. RICHARDSON PHOTO, DOW HELMERS COLLECTION

# VI | Tunnels, Highways, and Fading Whistles | 143

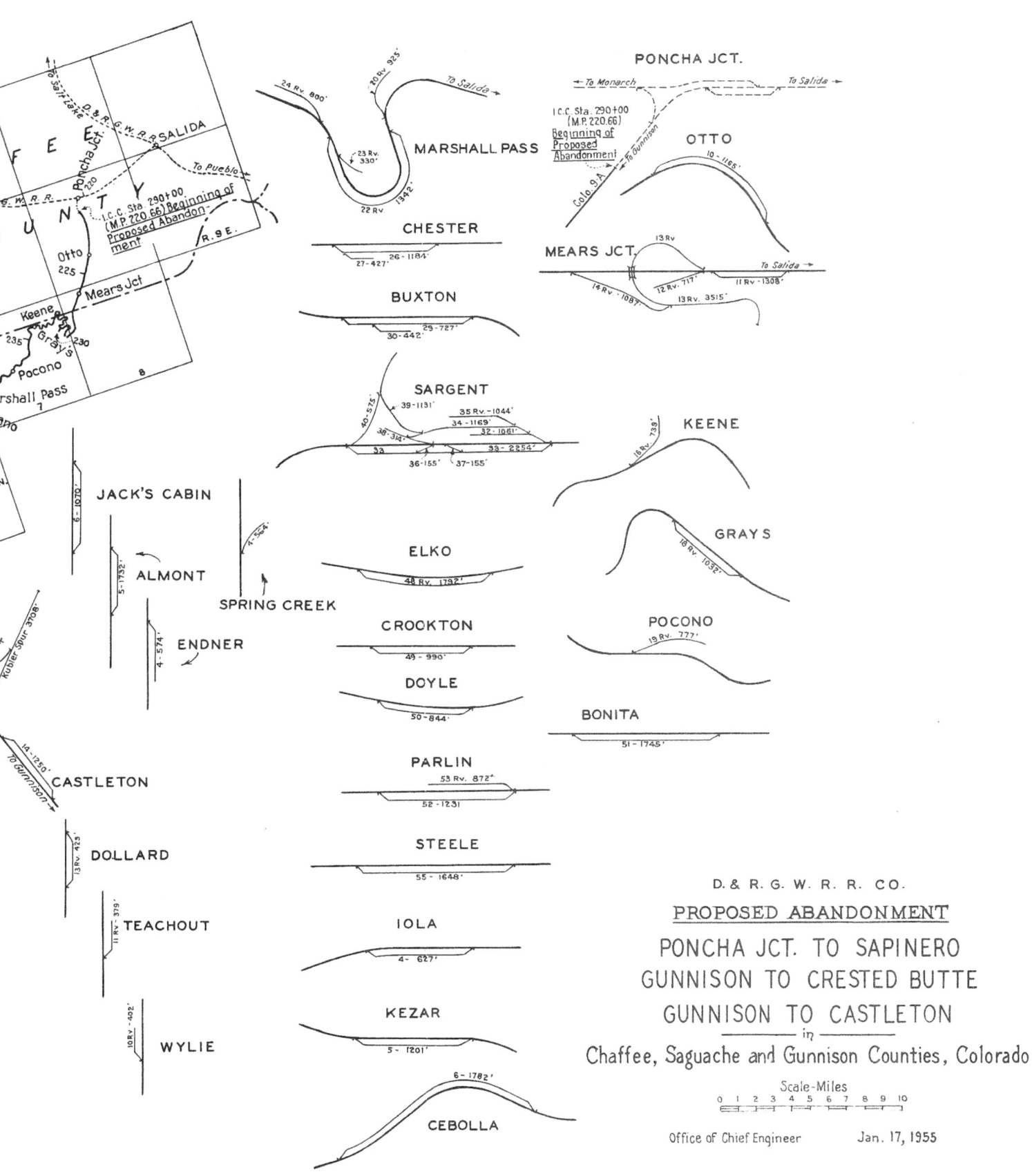

*Brinkerhoff Brothers Galloping Goose and dismantling equipment.*
NEAL R. MILLER PHOTO, DOW HELMERS COLLECTION

Still, there was hope that a renewal of mining activity at Crested Butte during the summer of 1953 might give the Rio Grande new incentive to reconsider or at least delay the abandonment. The *News-Champion* of August 27, 1953, reported that renewed activity at the Smith Hill Mine northeast of Crested Butte might give the railroad the shot in-the-arm it needed to stay out of the red.[37] Nevertheless, on September 29, Paul Albus recommended to the Interstate Commerce Commission that the line be discontinued on the basis of the hearing he had held in May.[38] Ten weeks later on December 9, the Commission authorized the Denver and Rio Grande to abandon the line from Salida to Gunnison and the branch lines out of Gunnison.[39] One last concession by the railroad was its agreement to pay the taxes that would have been due for 1954 and 1955 to Gunnison County. On paper the railroad over Marshall Pass was dead.

The physical end to the line came during the summer of 1955. With Engine No. 268 at its head, a wrecking train began to tear up the branch lines out of Gunnison to Sapinero, Baldwin, and Crested Butte. After three quarters of a century in service for the Rio Grande, which included displays at world fairs and a role in the movie "Denver and Rio Grande," Engine 268 was now the sad spectator to the destruction of the empire she had served so faithfully. Nostalgia gripped the townspeople of Gunnison and as the wrecking continued through the summer, they prepared a cement slab in Legion Park as the final resting place for the 268. By the second week in July, the line was torn up into Gunnison and on Saturday, July 16, at Gunnison's annual Pioneer Parade, the 268 was towed through the streets on a low-boy as the town said good-bye to the railroad that had served it for almost seventy-five years.[40] With the festivities over, Engine 268 sat on its rails at Legion Park while the No. 489 pulled the wrecking train eastward tearing up the track toward Marshall Pass.

By the end of August, the wrecking crew was past Sargent, leaving nothing but a deserted depot with a sagging front door which opened into a waiting room filled with dirt and cobwebs. Of all the towns across Marshall Pass only Sargent survived the passing of the railroad, and then only because of its strategic location on U.S. 50. The other Rio Grande stops, Chester, Shawano, Grays, and Shirley became only names in the memories of those who had once heard conductors pass through the cars intoning them. If the progress of the twentieth century demanded the removal of so vital a historical link, then it was appropriate that the men who undertook the project were conscious of the history that had passed beneath their wrecking train. The wrecking of the Marshall Pass line was done by the Brinkerhoff Brothers Construction Company of

*The rails disappear beneath the Shawano Tank whose spout will never again gush gallons of water into thirsty engines. Legend has it that Western State College of Gunnison fielded a "hard as iron" football team in the fall of 1955, because many of its members spent the preceding summer tearing up iron on Marshall Pass.*

ROBERT W. RICHARDSON PHOTO, DOW HELMERS COLLECTION

Rico, Colorado. Paul and Jack Brinkerhoff wrecked most of the Rio Grande Southern system in 1953 and 1954 and established a collection of pictures and artifacts from the project as well as keeping two of the famed Galloping Goose engines of the line. Now, on Marshall Pass, Paul Brinkerhoff observed, "Sure, we've made money pulling up these lines, but it makes you sort of sad when you figure that you wreck in a day a stretch that sometimes took weeks to build."

During the summer of 1955, the Brinkerhoffs pulled up 152 miles of narrow gauge track in the Gunnison country and over Marshall Pass. Originally, the operation was done by hand, but the Brinkerhoffs soon designed their own wrecker. It worked on an overhead pulley arrangement which lifted the rails and swung them into an open gondola car, instead of having to stack the rails by hand. Unlike the thirty-pound rails that were first laid in 1881, these rails now weighed eighty-five pounds to the yard. Ahead of the wrecker went men with sledgehammers knocking the rails loose, and then behind came men with buckets gathering up the spikes. Under the Brinkerhoff's contract, the Rio Grande retained the track, which they sold mostly for scrap, along with the buildings and water towers. The railroad also kept 35,000 of the ties. This left the Brinkerhoffs with an incredible 318,000 ties from the 1955 work which they sold for fence posts at thirty cents in place or fifty cents delivered. [41]

*The wrecking train pulls away from Shawano, entering the horseshoe curve, headed upgrade. Note the snowsheds, at extreme upper right, at the top of Marshall Pass.*

ROBERT W. RICHARDSON PHOTO, DOW HELMERS COLLECTION

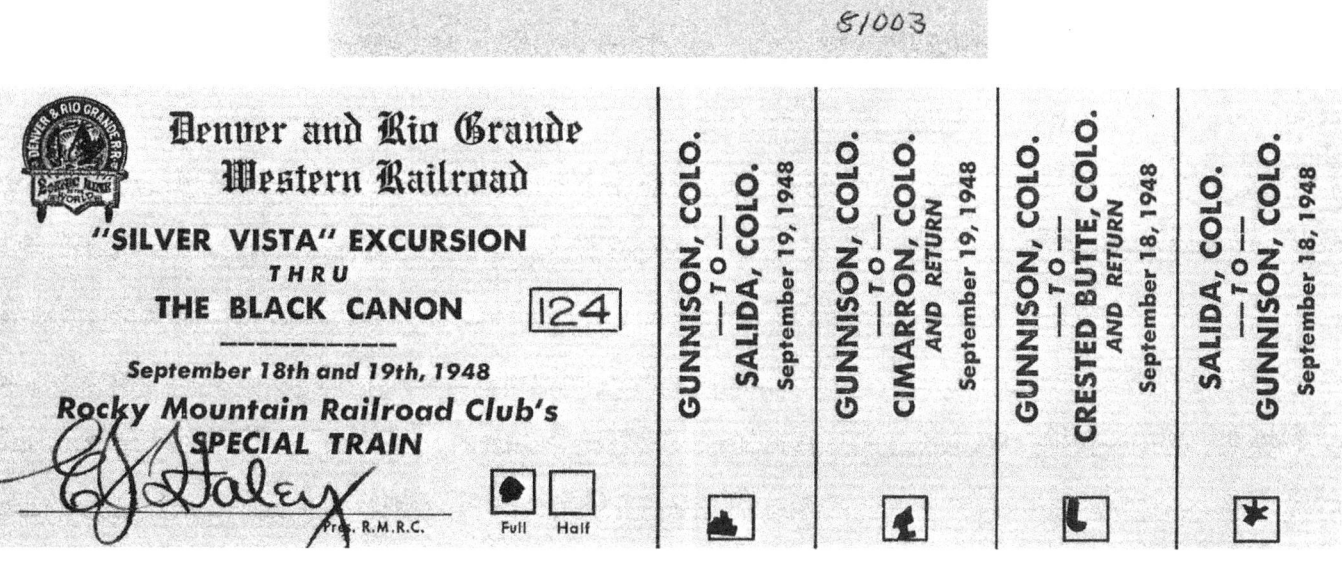

*Having become experienced hands at wrecking narrow gauge lines, the Brinkehroffs designed their own wrecker. It worked on an overhead pulley system which lifted the rails and swung them into an open gondola car, instead of having to stack the rails by hand.*   PAUL BRINKERHOFF

Throughout September, the Brinkerhoff train worked east over the pass. Ironically, the wrecking crew stayed at a hotel in Poncha Springs that had been built in 1879 and which had been used as quarters for some of the men building the railroad in 1881. The proprietors, Mr. and Mrs. Archie Gennow, still had registers dating back to that year. At six o'clock each morning during late September, Engine 489 whistled out of Mears Junction for another day of wrecking. As the end neared, the Brinkerhoffs were constantly besieged by narrow gauge railroad fans seeking one last ride to yesterday. The Brinkerhoffs began by taking a few, but soon the number mushroomed to such proportions that they simply had to refuse, except in the case of a few newspapermen who had come to write the obituary of an era.[42] By the first of October, almost on schedule, the job was done and the railroad line over Marshall Pass became history.

The railroad's demise did not, however, signal the passing of Marshall Pass into oblivion. Two events occurred that assured Marshall Pass of a continuing role in the commerce of central Colorado. In July of 1956, plans were announced to convert the roadbed, the rights to which had reverted back to the counties along the route, into a suitable auto road. Ranchers, forest service personnel, miners, and chamber of commerce officials were present at the July 11 meeting when the county commissioners of Saguache, Chaffee, and Gunnison Counties reached the decision. The decision was made primarily because of the promising development of uranium fields on the west side of the pass. Three companies were then at work in the region and were shipping ore. The companies were the Monarch Exploration Company, the Uncompahgre Uranium Company, and the Vulcan Silver-Lead Company, a subsidiary of Callahan Zinc-Lead

Company. Officials noted that putting the Marshall Pass road into shape would give the ore trucks a much more gentle grade than Monarch Pass. With the grading of the roadbed, Marshall Pass began to attract its first few automobile tourists.[43]

A second significant event for Marshall Pass was the construction of a gas line across the pass in 1962 by the Western Slope Gas Company. Originating in the Ignacio gas fields near Durango, the line ran up the San Luis Valley, crossed the Divide and dropped into Tank Seven, climbed Marshall Pass, and eventually reached Climax. The A. J. Curtis Pipeline Company was contracted for laying the line. The line from Tank Seven is an eight-inch pipe for approximately three miles to Mill Switch where it narrows to a six-inch pipe. The line follows the railroad grade most of the way, although it cuts directly across the big railroad loop above Chester at Mill Switch, and goes directly from Shawano to the summit instead of following the roadbed on its four-mile loop. Austin Clark, the Division Superintendent for Western Slope Gas, recalled that even though the mining trucks had been using the road off and on for six years, there were still many railroad spikes in the road which ruined many tires. The other major problem encountered was blasting through some of the cuts to gain the necessary depth for the pipe. A year later, in 1963, a six-inch line was built from Tank Seven into Gunnison.[44]

Mining activity on Marshall Pass never reached boom proportions, but throughout the 1960s, the road continued to attract an increasing number of summer tourists and railroad buffs. The road was passable, depending on the spring thaw, from May to whenever the snow closed it in late fall. By the 1970s, the railroad route over Marshall Pass seemed far removed from contemporary events. A trip over the pass would have saddened the men who once had

*August 13, 1955 Galloping Goose No. 7 and other contractor's equipment on the tail of the wye at Sargent.*
JACKSON THODE PHOTO, DOW HELMERS COLLECTION

*#489 gulps water at the Shawano tank before hauling a drag of scrap iron to the summit.*
ROBERT W. RICHARDSON PHOTO,
DOW HELMERS COLLECTION

battled the grades of the pass to get the trains through. Turning off U.S. 285 at Mears Junction, the road to the Lake O'Haver Campground in San Isabel National Forest parallels the old railroad grade running alongside Poncha Creek. The water tower from Mears Junction now stands in Pioneer Park in Gunnison as a companion to Engine 268. At Shirley, where only a few foundations remain, the railroad grade becomes the road and winds its way around the camp ground at O'Haver Lake. No sign is left of Keene, but one can notice the rapid growth of young aspen trees that have sprung up on both sides of the road since the railroad's demise. Grays Siding is little more than a swampy bog on one side of the road where grading has removed all signs of the water tower and siding. The one constant reminder of the small, black engines is the black streak of cinders which lies along the roadbed all of the way across the pass. Pocono, which one might have had trouble finding in 1890, is no longer even a wide spot in the road.

On the summit itself, the buildings and the snowsheds are gone, as are the buildings and lookout tower on the western slope. The grade of the summit siding is quite in evidence, running north from the big cut in the crest of the Divide. The only functioning facility

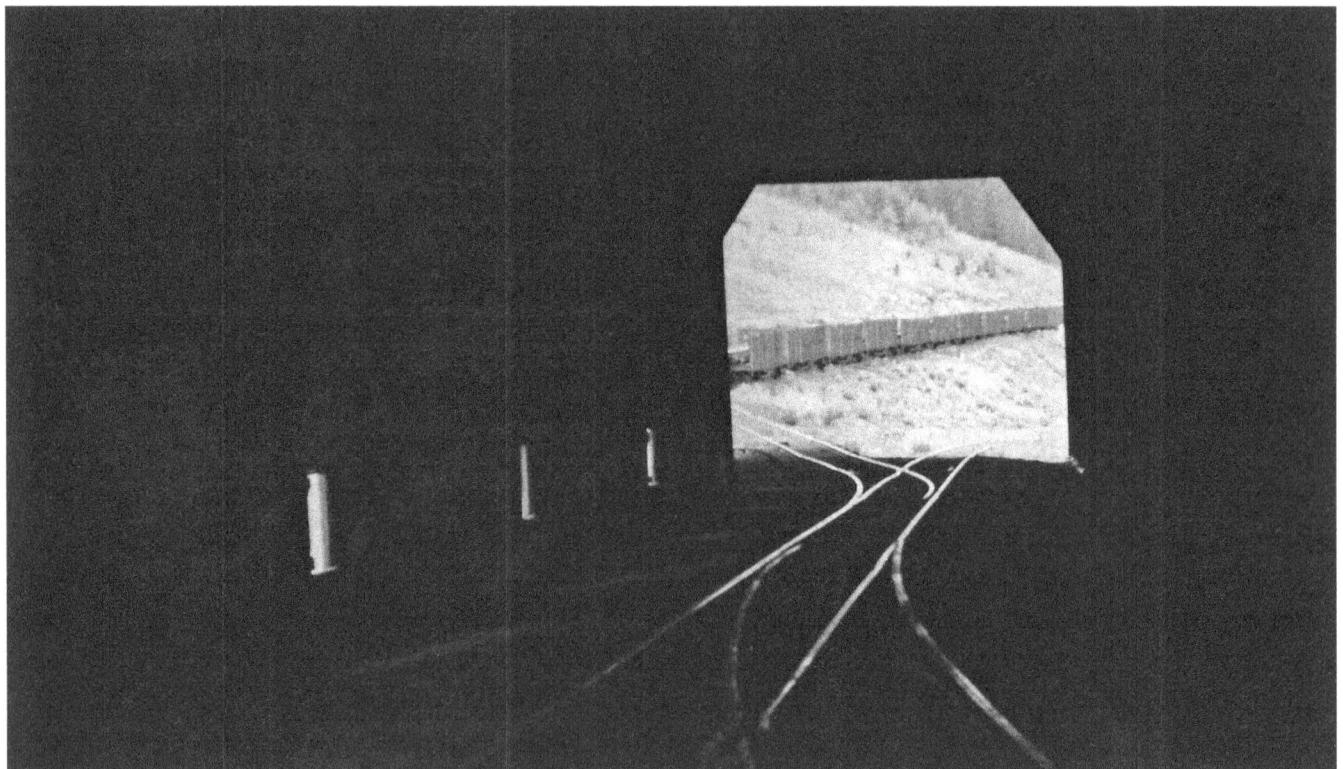

*A long drag of open-end gondolas stands on track 20 just outside the snowsheds on the east side of Marshall Pass in 1955. Mainline trackage drops away to the right.*
NEAL R. MILLER PHOTO, DOW HELMERS COLLECTION

*This was, perhaps, the final photo made of the top of Marshall Pass, taken just a few days prior to the removal of the iron. September, 1955.*   Robert W. Richardson photo, Dow Helmers Collection

remaining on the summit is the water diversion ditch. The ditch gathers water on the higher, western slopes of Mount Ouray and then channels it over the pass into the waters of Poncha Creek. The ditch was constructed in the days of the Colorado Fuel and Iron Corporation's affiliation with the Rio Grande so the corporation could take more water from the Arkansas River in Pueblo. This ditch may be the first example of trans-mountain diversion in Colorado. Recently, plans have been discussed to construct a diversion tunnel through the Marshall Pass area to divert water from the Tomichi watershed to the San Luis Valley.

On the west side of the pass, Shawano is the point where the Western Slope Gas Company's pipeline leaves the roadbed and goes directly east to the summit. Chester is still a wide spot in the road where a camper or two can usually be found in the summer. To the north of Chester a road leads to the old Pinnacle Mine of the 1950s uranium boom. During 1978, an Environmental Impact Statement was filed by the Homestake Mining Company which would again bring mining activity to the Pinnacle area in the form of an open pit uranium mine.

At Tank Seven, the railroad grade goes off into the pasture lands and a county road takes traffic into Sargent. The foundation blocks of the Tank Seven tower are still in place as are several decaying buildings. Buxton is now overgrown with weeds, and cattle graze along the road bed. At Sargent, the water tower still stands although in poor condition. The Sargent depot was moved to Gunnison in 1976 through the efforts of the Gunnison County Pioneer and Historical Society. The building joined #268 in Pioneer Park and has been restored to house the Society's considerable collection of railroad memorabilia. The yards where helper engines once busily moved about are deserted and overgrown with weeds. The town is little more than a quiet village today. Indeed, an era has ended.

Yet, who is to say that one cannot stand quietly on the summit of the pass and see the deserted main line come alive with frenzied activity as a small, black engine with whistle screaming comes steaming around a curve once more climbing Marshall Pass?

[1] *Gunnison News-Champion*, November 7, 1913, p. 1.
[2] Athearn, *Rebel of the Rockies*, p. 221.
[3] *Gunnison News-Champion*, January 31, 1919, p. 1.
[4] *Ibid.*, February 21, 1919, p. 1.
[5] *Ibid.*, April 11, 1919, p. 1.
[6] *Ibid.*, April 25, 1919, p. 1.
[7] *Ibid.*, May 2, 1919, p. 1.
[8] *Ibid.*, October 17, 1919, p. 1.
[9] *Ibid.*, November 21, 1919, p. 1.
[10] *Ibid.*, December 26, 1919, p. 1.
[11] *Ibid.*, January 16, 1920, p. 1.
[12] *Ibid.*, March 5, 1920, p. 1.
[13] Athearn, *Rebel of the Rockies*, pp. 266-7.
[14] *Gunnison News-Champion*, November 5, 1920, p. 1.

*"'The torch of iniquity!" The vicious hiss of the acetylene torch conclusively punctured the end of the iron trail over Marshall Pass. Workman preparing for removal of the rails at east end of the snowsheds.*
NEAL R. MILLER PHOTO, DOW HELMERS COLLECTION

[15] *Ibid.*, July 7, 1923, p. 1.

[16] *Ibid.*, February 17, 1938, p. 6.

[17] Duane Vandenbusche, Interview with Rial Lake, September 20, 1968.

[18] *Pueblo Chieftain*, August 15, 1971, Section C, p. 1.

[19] *Gunnison News-Champion*, February 6, 1936, p. 10.

[20] *Ibid.*, May 28, 1936, p. 1.

[21] *Ibid.*, June 18, 1936, p. 1.

[22] *Ibid.*, July 23, 1936, p. 1.

[23] *Ibid.*, December 3, 1936, p. 1.

[24] *Ibid.*, December 31, 1936, p. 1.

[25] *Ibid.*, January 28, 1937, p. 3.

[26] *Ibid.*, February 4, 1937, p. 1.

[27] *Ibid.*, June 17, 1937, p. 1.

[28] *Pueblo Chieftain*, August 15, 1971, Section C, p. 1.

[29] *Gunnison News-Champion*, July 2, 1936, p. 1.

[30] *Ibid.*, September 26, 1940, p. 1.

[31] *Ibid.*, November 7, 1940, p. 1.

[32] *Ibid.*, November 21, 1940, p. 1.

[33] *Rocky Mountain News*, July 23, 1941, p. 9.

[34] *Interview with Dr. Kenneth J. Lampert*, November 24, 1973.

[35] *Gunnison News-Champion*, May 28, 1953, p. 1.

[36] *New York Times*, October 4, 1953, Section F, p. 1.

[37] *Gunnison News-Champion*, October 1, 1953, p. 1.

[38] *Ibid.*, October 1, 1953, p. 1.

[39] *Ibid.*, December 10, 1953, p. 1.

[40] *Ibid.*, July 20, 1955, p. 1.

[41] *Canon City Daily Record*, September 19, 1955, p. 1.

[42] *Ibid.*, September 20, 1955, p. 1.

[43] *Ibid.*, July 13, 1956, p. 1.

[44] Letter to Author from Austin L. Clark, Division Superintendent of Western Slope Gas Company, October 29, 1973.

*The summit buildings, looking west, just prior to consigning these structures to oblivion in August, 1955.*
NEAL R. MILLER PHOTO, DOW HELMERS COLLECTION

*The roof tops of Marshall Pass. These cover the cut and the railroad buildings on the west side of the cut, including the great turntable and the Marshall Pass Post Office.*
JAMES OZMENT PHOTO, DOW HELMERS COLLECTION

*Remnants of a bygone era—stone bridge abutments still stand, where the Marshall Pass line crossed Poncha Creek, not far above Mears Junction.*　　　　　　　　　　　　　　　　　　　　　　　　　DOW HELMERS COLLECTION

*About a mile from Poncha Springs, en route to Poncha and Marshall Passes, can be seen lengthy stretches of the abandoned right-of-way. Much of this grade was supported by walls of stonework, so carefully fashioned and fitted that no mortar was needed.*　　　　　　　　　　　　　　　　　　　　　　　　　DOW HELMERS COLLECTION

*"Prelude to magnificence" was the feeling travelers got when their little trains turned up Poncha Creek toward Marshall Pass here at Mears Junction, marked in 1968 only by the old water tank.*   DOW HELMERS COLLECTION

*Looking downgrade to the Mears Junction tank along the abandoned right of way, 1967.*

DOW HELMERS COLLECTION

*"The Agony of Abandonment" of the snowsheds on Marshall—little by little the skeleton becomes exposed. The rails are gone—hope is gone. Looking out the east end.*

JAMES L. OZMENT PHOTO, DOW HELMERS COLLECTION

*Snow fences were built along the track to protect it from blowing and drifting snow. The most substantial fence was located on a big curve on the four-mile loop, halfway between Shawano and the summit. Braced to withstand the fierce westerly winds, portions of the fence still stand today.*

AUTHOR'S COLLECTION

*In July, 1957, Neal R. Miller made this photograph of the desolation on Marshall Pass. The railroad grade curves through center. The building at left was the station, at right, the coal chute. At extreme right is the debris-filled pit of the turntable.*                    NEAL R. MILLER PHOTO, DOW HELMERS COLLECTION

*Looking west from the summit crest shortly after abandonment, across the debris-filled turntable pit to the depot and post office (left) and the coal bin.*                    JAMES L. OZMENT PHOTO, DOW HELMERS COLLECTION

VI | TUNNELS, HIGHWAYS, AND FADING WHISTLES | 159

*Gus Latham came to the top of Marshall Pass in 1930 as a section worker, and in the late 1960s wound up owning the only two structures then standing on the pass—these two section houses. Latham spent the summers living here.*
DOW HELMERS COLLECTION

*In the middle background, the cut through the Continental Divide lies barren in 1968, long since stripped of its protective snowshed. To the left of the cut are the remains of the old toll road.*
DOW HELMERS COLLECTION

*This extraordinary picture, made from the top of Marshall Pass looking west, encompasses many, many miles of the railroad grade, as it enters the picture at right center, makes the great loop at the Shawano water tank, and continues downgrade towards Sargent.*
NEAL R. MILLER PHOTO, DOW HELMERS COLLECTION

*From the summit down to Shawano was only 700 vertical feet, but the railroad required four miles of circuitous grade to negotiate the elevation difference.*
NEAL R. MILLER PHOTO, DOW HELMERS COLLECTION

# VI | Tunnels, Highways, and Fading Whistles

*A fine hand must go to R. Omar Richardson who snapped this classic picture as the author banked a Cessna 172 over the summit of the pass. The main line can be seen coming up the western slope, crossing the Continental Divide through the deep cut, and descending past two remaining buildings on the east side. Also visible is the Western Slope Gas Company pipeline cut running up from Shawano, the ruins of the watchtower and buildings, the grade of the summit siding, and the cut of the Colorado Fuel and Iron Steel Corporation's water diversion ditch.*
R. OMAR RICHARDSON PHOTO

*The cut through the Continental Divide, at the crest of Marshall Pass.*
DOW HELMERS COLLECTION

*West from the summit across the weed-choked pit of the summit turntable, 1968.*

DOW HELMERS COLLECTION

*Tank Seven, circa 1968, before the removal of the water tank, looking upgrade.*

DOW HELMERS COLLECTION

VI | TUNNELS, HIGHWAYS, AND FADING WHISTLES | 163 |

"Station P 36" better known as "Tank Seven," 6.4 miles east of Sargent, at the start of the very steep grade up Marshall Pass. The cinders are deep along the abandoned right-of-way, attesting to the power needed to move trains upgrade.
DOW HELMERS COLLECTION

Windowless, clothed in peeling paint, utterly forlorn, the Sargent depot nevertheless stands with dignity and pride—ready at a moment's notice to welcome back the dispatcher to his position of authority in the front of the station.
DOW HELMERS COLLECTION

*Although it has been many years since a stalwart little narrow gauge locomotive has whistled for Sargent, the Rio Grande water tank still dominates the picturesque little mountain village, located at the western foot of both Monarch and Marshall Passes. (1967)*   DOW HELMERS COLLECTION

*Engine 268, flanger and cars in yard at Pioneer Museum, Gunnison.*   DOW HELMERS COLLECTION

VI | Tunnels, Highways, and Fading Whistles | 165

*In August of 1978, only a few bulldozer ruts mark the location of the summit buildings.*
Author's Collection

*Thanks to the efforts of Gunnison businessmen, the water tower from Mears Junction now stands beside #268 and a string of cars on the grounds of the Pioneer Museum in Gunnison. The contraption in the foreground is the top of a flanger.*
Author's Collection

*In August of 1978, only the loading platform for ore from several mines on Mount Ouray remains intact on the summit. Hidden in the grove of trees to the right, a fleet of motor homes park where once black locomotives hissed their steamy breath.*　　　　　　　　　　　　　　　　　　　　　　　　　　　　　　　　　AUTHOR'S COLLECTION

# Epilogue

# A Glorious Past, An Uncertain Future

*"The Agony and the Ecstasy" of mountain railroading, dramatized as few pictures have ever done. Engine 489 spews steam and smoke into the skies, toiling mightily to surmount the great Continental Divide with a long merchandise drag.*
ROBERT. W. RICHARDSON PHOTO, DOW HELMERS COLLECTION

# Epilogue | A Glorious Past, An Uncertain Future

It has been over one hundred years since William Marshall first forced his way across the pass now bearing his name. Certainly the impact of the pass on the development of Colorado during that century was a major one. In 1873, the Western Slope of Colorado was undeveloped and largely unexplored, a land of Chief Ouray and his Utes. Marshall's presence in western Colorado with the Wheeler Survey signaled an awakening of interest in the great and seemingly endless land west of the Front Range. A year after Marshall made his painful journey to Denver with his toothache, Sylvester Richardson established a permanent settlement at Gunnison. Within a few years, rich mineral strikes in the San Juans and Elk Mountains heralded the beginnings of a tidal wave of prospectors spilling westward across the Continental Divide, the vanguard of an approaching civilization. The prospectors came to the Western Slope and the Gunnison country by the Indians's favorite route across Cochetopa Pass; they came across the rough and rocky passes of the Taylor Park region, Williams, Cottonwood, and Tincup; but mostly they came across Marshall Pass.

No route into the Gunnison country influenced the region as much as Marshall Pass. In 1880, its gentle grades and Mears's toll road provided the best crossing of the Continental Divide for stagecoaches and freight wagons. By the end of that year, the pass was the main artery of commerce and transportation between the entire Gunnison Valley and the railroads east of the Divide. With the arrival of Palmer's Denver and Rio Grande Railway in August of 1881, this main artery became the cornerstone of the region's commerce and transportation. At last the mines had a cheap and direct route to the markets of the Eastern Slope. By 1883, the line across Marshall Pass was the only line with transcontinental connections through Colorado. During the crucial growing decade of the 1880s, the railroads were tied explicitly to the growth of Colorado. The promising Gunnison country sat on the main line and grew with the state.

Although eclipsed by the standard gauge route across Tennessee Pass in 1890, the Marshall Pass line shrugged off the competition and became even more closely tied to the regional development of the Western Slope. It was well into the twentieth century before Monarch and Cochetopa Passes stayed open throughout the winter. During those long winters it was the narrow gauge across Marshall Pass that provided the Gunnison country with supplies and contacts with the outside world. Unfortunately, politics dealt Marshall Pass a dirty blow on several occasions. Ten thousand more votes at the 1920 tri-tunnel election and a favorable Charles Vail would have led to a broad gauge railroad tunnel and a national highway.

As the early decades of the twentieth century rolled by, politics dictated that Marshall Pass give up its cornerstone role in Colorado commerce. Thus, the pass made the slow transition into nostalgia and history. Now, a century after William Marshall's discovery, only a tourist road remains to boast of a glorious past. Perhaps in the stillness of the summit station it does seem as though the pass has come full circle back to the days of William Marshall. Yet, there are those who look at the pass and see, just as Marshall did, the low elevation, favorable grade, and gentle slopes. In 1873, William Marshall imagined narrow gauge locomotives chugging up the grades of Marshall Pass. A century later, enterprising, twentieth century William Jackson Palmers may see the pass as an avenue of mass transportation monorails and super trains speeding products and passengers across the state and nation. While the land of the Gunnison country requires careful control over development, its potential in recreational facilities and mineral resources is vast. It is not too surprising or speculative to imagine Marshall Pass once more catapulted back

# Epilogue | A Glorious Past, An Uncertain Future

into the center of Colorado commerce and transportation as an artery to serve the Gunnison country during the development of these resources.

The history of Marshall Pass tells of a glorious past tied to the development of Colorado from a rough and dusty frontier to a recreational and industrial giant. For the present, the pass lies quiet in a state of transition; yet, while its immediate future remains uncertain, a spark remains from that glorious past which seems to herald a promising future for William Marshall's pass.

*AUTHOR'S NOTE – This epilogue was written with the main manuscript in 1974. Now, some six years later in 1980, the future of Marshall Pass and the entire Gunnison country stands at a critical watershed. Competing interests for natural resources, which include a gargantuan open pit uranium mine and accompanying tailings pond on the western slope of Marshall Pass, promise controversy and confrontation. Now, as in 1880, the winds across Marshall Pass cry out that the land is on the threshold of dramatic and unsettling change.*

*AUTHOR'S NOTE 2020 – Forty years have passed since this book was first published and almost fifty years since I wrote my first words about Marshall Pass for a freshman English class at Western State College. Some of the things I envisioned then for Colorado have not come to pass. There are no high-speed rail links throughout the state and even the Rio Grande's standard gauge line over Tennessee Pass has been abandoned. The Homestake uranium mine operated for a time, but has been closed for decades. Perhaps the biggest change atop the pass in recent years is that the Colorado Trail between Denver and Durango, as well as the Continental Divide National Scenic Trail, crosses the ridgeline below which William Marshall huddled in 1873. Given the huge influx of population and multiple uses that Colorado faces in the twenty-first century, a peaceful ramble across Marshall Pass may be victory enough.*

# SELECTED BIBLIOGRAPHY

### ARTICLES
Cummins, D. H. "Toll Roads in Southwestern Colorado." *The Colorado Magazine*, XXIX (April, 1952), 104.

Chappell, Gordon. "Scenic Line of the World." *The Colorado Rail Annual*, VIII (1970), pp. 10-76.

Dawson, Thomas, "Godfather of Marshall Pass." *The Trail*, September, 1920, pp. 6-10. (Based on personal interview with William Marshall).

Hafen, Leroy. "Otto Mears, 'Pathfinder of the San Juan.'" *The Colorado Magazine*, IX, No. 2 (March, 1932), 71.

Rockwell, Wilson. "Portrait in the Gallery, Otto Mears, Pathfinder of the San Juans." *Denver Westerners Brand Book*, XXX (1967), 3-24.

Stevens, H. W. "Adventure on the High Iron." *Esquire*, October, 1946, p. 87.

### BOOKS
Anderson, George L. *General William J. Palmer, A Decade of Colorado Railroad Building, 1870-1880.* Colorado Springs: Colorado College Publications, 1936.

Athearn, Robert G. *Rebel of the Rockies.* New Haven, Connecticut: Yale University Press, 1962.

Bartlett, Richard Adams, *Great Surveys of the American West.* Norman, Oklahoma: University of Oklahoma Press, 1962.

Beebe, Lucius, and Clegg, Charles. *Narrow Gauge in the Rockies.* Berkeley: Howell-North, 1958.

Crofutt, George A. *Crofutt's Overland Tours.* Chicago: Arthur H. Day & Co., Publishers, 1888.

Ellis, Amanda. *Legends and Tales of the Rockies.* Colorado Springs: Denton Printing Company, 1954.

Everett, George G. *The Cavalcade of Railroads in Central Colorado.* Denver: Golden Bell Press, 1966.

Ingersoll, Ernest. *The Crest of the Continent: A Record of a Summer's Ramble in the Rocky Mountains and Beyond.* Glorieta, New Mexico: The Rio Grande Press, Inc., 1969. (Recount of 1883 Colorado tour).

Lathrop, Gilbert A. *Little Engines and Big Men.* Caldwell, Idaho: Caxton Printers, Ltd., 1954. (Based on personal railroad experiences).

Poor, M. C. Denver, *South Park and Pacific, A History of the Denver, South Park and Pacific Railroad and Allied Narrow Gauge Lines of the Colorado and Southern Railway Co.* Denver: World Press (Rocky Mountain Railroad Club), 1949.

Sprague, Marshall. *The Great Gates, The Story of the Rocky Mountain Passes.* Boston: Little, Brown and Company, 1964.

Strahorn, Carrie Adell. *Fifteen Thousand Miles by Stage.* New York: The Knickerbocker Press, 1915.

Wallace, Betty. *Gunnison Country.* Denver: Sage Books, 1960.

Warman, Cy. *Tales of an Engineer.* New York: Charles Scribner's Sons, 1897.

### LETTERS, PERSONAL PAPERS, AND MANUSCRIPTS
*In Letters to the Author*

Clark, Austin L., Division Superintendent of Western Slope Gas Company, Salida, October 29, 1973.

*In the State Historical Society of Colorado Library, Denver*

Denver and Rio Grande Archives, No. 32658. "Summary of Construction of Denver and Rio Grande Railway to and within Gunnison Country."

Denver and Rio Grande Archives, No. 4307. "Letter, H. P. Bennet to H. A. Risley, April 27, 1882." (Details of Toll Road sale).

Denver and Rio Grande Time-Table, Salida and Gunnison—First District, July 30, 1893.

William Jackson Palmer Papers.

Robert F. Weitbrec Papers.

### NEWSPAPERS
*Canon City Daily Record*, 1955-1956.
*Denver Times*, 1902.
*Gunnison Daily News-Democrat*, 1881-1885.
*Gunnison Daily Review-Press*, 1882.
*Gunnison News*, 1880-1881. (Becomes *Gunnison News-Democrat*).
*Gunnison News-Champion*, 1901-1955.
*Gunnison News-Democrat*, 1881-1891.
*Gunnison Review*, 1880-1882. (Becomes *Gunnison Review-Press*).
*Gunnison Review-Press*, 1882-1890.
*Gunnison Republican*, 1901-1903.
*Gunnison Tribune*, 1891, 1903.
*Mountain Mail*, (Salida, Colorado), 1880-1882.
*New York Times*, 1953.
*Pueblo Chieftain*, 1971.

*Rocky Mountain News*, 1941.
*The Solid Muldoon*. (Ouray, Colorado), 1880.

## UNPUBLISHED DISSERTATIONS AND THESES

Cummins, D. H. "A Social and Economic History of Southwestern Colorado, 1860-1948." Unpublished Ph.D. dissertation, University of Texas, 1951.

Wallace, Betty. "Six Beans in the Wheel." Unpublished Master's Thesis, Western State College of Colorado, 1956.

*The depot at Sargent, which once hummed with activity, quiet and deserted before its removal to Gunnison. The snow almost to the top of the fence posts and the darkened interior suggest that it will indeed be a long wait for anyone entering the door marked "Waiting Room".*　　　　　AUTHOR'S COLLECTION

*From above Mill Switch the view looks west, downgrade to Sargent, extreme background right. The roadbed splits in the foreground, just above Tank Seven with the railroad grade running left through fields and the county road right on into Sargent.*
DOW HELMERS COLLECTION

# INDEX

*Photos in Italics*

Adams, Charles, 136
Albus, Paul, 141, 144
Alpine Tunnel, 32, 49, 67, 96, 99-100, 128
    construction, 33, 37, 48
altitude records, 99-100
Altman Pass, 32, 127
Ammons, Teller, 134, 136
Ashley, Frank, 132
Atchison, Topeka, and Santa Fe Railroad, 26
Ausmus, Bill, 111, 113-116

Barlow and Sanderson Stage Company
    (later J. L. Sanderson and Company), 15, 30, 32, 37
Bartlett, H. C., 121, 128
Bartlett, Richard, 13
Basswell, Bert, 86
Beebe, Lucius, 82
Beeler, Cy, 97
Black, Robert C. III, 62
Boyle, Hal, 104
Brinkerhoff Brothers, Construction Company, 145
Brinkerhoff, Jack, 146
Brinkerhoff, Paul, 146
broad-gauging, 65, 77, 118, 120
Bush, Benjamin F., 77, 118
Buxton, 56, 151

Canon City, 27
Carter, Carroll M., 121, 128
Chester, 56, 71, 84, *113*, 151
Clark, Austin, 149
Cleora, 39
Cochetopa Pass, 13, 36, 136
Colorado Springs, 24
Colorado Trail, 169
Continental Divide National Scenic Trail, 169
Cooley, O. D. "Oz," 82, 92
Cowden, R. E., 133
*Crest of the Continent,* 30, 56, 61-64
Crested Butte, 29, 43, 46, 141, 144
Crofutt, George, 56
Cross, Jacob, 41
Cross, James, 41
Crylie, William, 104

Darby, Ruth, 132
Davis, Ed, 88
Day, David, 20
de Pret, Phillipe, 132

*Denver and Rio Grande* (movie), 144
Denver and Rio Grande Railway, 9, 17
    arrival in Gunnison, 24, 42-43, 46
    incorporation, 25-26
    reasons for narrow gauge, 26
    reasons to build over Marshall Pass, 28-29
    timetables, 60, 67-68, 73
    workers, 34-35
Denver and Rio Grande Western Railroad, 141
Denver and Rio Grande Western Railway, 46
Denver and Salt Lake Railroad, 121, 128
Denver, South Park, and Pacific Railroad, 9, 67, 96
    arrival in Gunnison, 48-49
    competition with D&RG, 75
    incorporation, 27
*Denver Times,* 75
*Denver Tribune,* 40
Dobbie, Tom, 92
Dodge, D.C., 12, 32
Dotsero Cutoff, 121, 128

Edwards, Nelson, 86-87
Evans, James A., 33
Evans, John, 9, 27
Evans, William G., 123

*Fifteen Thousand Miles by Stage,* 17
flanger plow, 95
Flynn, T. J., 132
Fort Garland, 14

Galloping Goose, *144*, 146, *149*
Gast, Dave, 88
Gennow, Archie, 148
Gilpin, William, 14
Gimlett, Frank, 46, 97, 104
Gist, Thomas, 75
Goldwater, Harry, 88
Gould, Jay, 27, 49
Grant, U.S., 75
Gray, Homer, 133
Grays Siding, 36, 53, 56, 71, 85, 150
*Great Surveys of the American West,* 13
Green and Foody, 37
Gregg, Merle, 82, 105-107
Groff, Charles, 42
Groswald, Thomas, 132
Gunnison, 15, 16, 19, 21, 27-28, 30, 37, 39, 42, 49, *76*, 164
Gunnison Chamber of Commerce, 133
Gunnison Hotel, 19

*Gunnison News*, 15, 16, 20, 30, 32
*Gunnison News-Champion*, 71, 77, 92, 121, 128, 129, 134, 135-138, 144
*Gunnison News-Democrat*, 37, 47
*Gunnison Republican*, 90
*Gunnison Review*, 12, 16, 17, 24, 27, 36, 37, 40
*Gunnison Review-Press*, 95
*Gunnison Tribune*, 84

*Harper's Weekly*, 65
Haverly, J. H., 42
Hayden, Ferdinand Vandeveer, 12
Helmers, Dow, 104, *105*
Hendricks, Margaret, 107
Hetherington, George, 121
Highway 50 Association, 134
Hill, Nathaniel P., 21
Homestake Mining Company, 151
Hooper, Shadrach K., 64
Humphreys, A. A., 12
Hunt, Alexander, 26, 40

Ingersoll, Ernest, 30, 56, 61-64, 99

Jackson Spur, 56
Jackson, William Henry, 31, 39, 64
Johnson, Edward C., 132-134
Jordan, Bill, 92
Jull, Orange, 96
Jull plow, 96

Kansas Pacific Railroad, 25
Kearns, Billy, 98-99
Keene, 53, 150
Kerndt, Leslie, 92
Kipling, Rudyard, 64, 104
Koontz, Gary, *100*
Kuhler, Otto, 62

Laird, George W., 118
Lake City, 46
Lake O'Haver Campground, 150
Lake, Rial, 131
Lamborn, R. Henry, 26
La Veta Pass 26
Latham, Gus, 109-111, 141
Lathrop, Gilbert, 85, 90
Leadville 9, 14
    arrival of D&RG, 17, 21, 27
Lindsey, E. E., 92
*Life is Like a Mountain Railroad*, 92
*Little Engines and Big Men*, 85, 90
Lory, Charles, 123

Marshall, Charles A., 12
Marshall Creek, 12, *130*
Marshall Pass, 12
    abandonment, 140-145
    accidents, 42, 48, 83-88, *92-93*
    automobiles, 75, 129, 132, 148-149
    descriptions of travel over, 17-19, 61-64, 104, 138-139
    discovery 13-14
    helper engines, 88, 90
    highway controversy, 132-137
    holdup, 71-72
    railroad construction technique, 24, *27*
    ski trains, 131-132
    snow fences, 94-95, *97, 157*
    snow operations, 93-99
    snowsheds, 46-47, 48, 49, *63*, 67, 94, *112, 135, 140, 141, 150, 157*
    summit, *31, 38, 39, 40, 56, 64, 70, 72, 114, 127, 137, 139, 151*, 154, *158-159, 161, 164*
    telegraph, 21
    toll road, 15-19
    tunnel, 76-77, 120-121, 123-124, 127
    water diversion ditch, 151
Marshall Pass and Gunnison Toll Road, 15, 17, *18*, 19, 29, 31, 36, 132
Marshall Pass Post Office, 109-110, 141
Marshall, Phoebe, 12
Marshall, Thomas, 12
Marshall, William Louis, *13*, 36, 93, 168
    career, 12
    discovery of pass, 13-14
    request for railroad pass, 52-53
    toothache, 13
McCanne, D. J., 68, 71
McDermott, Wes, 131
McDowell, Ted, 104
McKee family, 15
McMurtrie, James, 31, 49
Mears, Dave, 13, 53
Mears, Otto, 13, *14*, 50, 53, 132
    background, 14
    toll road construction, 13-17, 29, 31
    toll road profits, 19-20
Mears Junction, 15, *33*, 34, 35, *52*, 53, *80, 119, 126*, 134, *150, 156*
Mellen, William Proctor, 25, 26
Mexican National Railway, 26
Mill Switch, 71, 149
Moffat Tunnel, 120-121, 123
Monarch Pass, 30-31, 121, 123, 127, 132, 137, 138
Moriarty, T. K., 141
*Mountain Mail* (Salida), 15, 32, 34, 36, 84, 93
Mudge, Henry U., 90-91

Myers, J. C., 47, 94
Myers, Marion, 72

Nathrop, George, 132
Nelson, Andy, 98-99
Nelson, Starr, 88
Nelson, W. H., 132-133, 137
*New York Times*, 65

Orman, James, 72
Otto, 44, 53, *119, 122*
Owens, George, 30
Owens Sawmill, 34
Ouray, Chief, 12
Ouray Creek, 37
Ouray, Mount, *11*, 12, *31, 133*
Outcalt, W. M., 15

Palmer, Mary "Queen" Lincoln Mellen, 24, 25
Palmer, William Jackson, 9, 23, 24, 46, 65
    background, 25,
    incorporates D&RG, 25-26
    town development, 39
Parlin, 41
Parlin, Frank, 92
Perkins, Frank, 85
Pinnacle mine, 151
Pitkin, Frederick, 21
Pocono, 56
Poncha Creek, 12, 56, *102, 155*
Poncha Pass, 14, 26, 32, *132*
Poncha Pass Toll Road, 15
Poncha Springs, 30, 32, 34, 53, 148
Powell, John Wesley, 12
Public Utilities Commission, 138
Pyle, Ernie, 138-139

Raton Pass, 9, 26
Reardon, Tom, 90-91
Reynolds, A. E., 123
Richardson, R. Omar, *100*
Richardson, Sylvester, 19
Ridgway, Arthur, 71
Rio Grande Southern, 146
*Rocky Mountain News*, 124
Rocky Mountain Railroad Club special, *132, 133, 136,*
    140
rotary plows, *84*, 95
Royal Gorge, 9, 26, 27, 29, 127
Ruland, John, 71
Ryan, Paddy, 85-86

Saguache, 14, 136
St. Elmo, 32
Salida, 29, 30, 32, 34, 39, *67, 68, 88*, 125
San Juan Mountains, 12, 13, 14, 29, 46
San Luis Valley, 12, 13, 26, 32
Sargent, 40-41, 56, 58, *59, 103, 129, 138*, 151, *163, 164*
Sargents, Joseph, 56
Schuyler, Howard J., 26
Seeley, Frank, 48
Shaw, Charles, 86
Shawano, *41*, 56, *70, 74, 77, 91*, 92, *145, 146, 150*, 151,
    *160*
"*Shawano*" (train), *119-124*, 138
Shawano Loop, 56, 65, *74, 75*
Shirley, *35, 36, 37*, 53, *55, 87, 90*, 150
Shores, "Doc," 49
Shoup, Oliver, 123
*Solid Muldoon*, 20
South Arkansas (Salida), 15, 16
Sprague, Marshall, 9
Stevens, H. W., 82
Stevens, John F., 118
Strahorn, Carrie Adell, 17-19
Sweitzer, Charles, 131

Taft, William Howard, 75
Tank Seven, 56, 84, *115*, 131, 149, 151, *162, 163*
Tank Seven Creek, *130*
third rail, 65, *125*
Tennessee Pass, 46, 65-66, 77, 79, 100
Treaty of Boston, 26

uranium mining, 148-149, 169

Vail, Charles, 133-137
Van Pelt, Nelson, 88
Veo, Frank, 108

Warman, Cy, 96
wedge plows, 95
Weitbrec, Robert F., 30-31, 34-35, 41
Western Slope Gas Company, 149
Westmoreland Coal Company, 25
Wheeler, George Montague, 12
Wheeler Survey, 12-13
Wilcox, Horace, 124